THE RECOVERY OF *love*

LIVING IN A TROUBLED WORLD

DAVID CADMAN

THE RECOVERY OF *love*

DAVID CADMAN

ISBN: 9798841614104

HOSTED BY:

The Guerrand-Hermès Foundation for Peace, The University of Wales Trinity St David's Harmony Institute and The Spirit of Humanity Forum, as part of *A Narrative of Love.*

Funding for this book has kindly been provided by the Pureland Foundation.

As a sequel to *Love and the Divine Feminine,* published by Panacea Books in 2020.

The Image on the next page, on the front and the back cover and elsewhere in this book, originally drawn by Beth Lewis, is taken from the Great Tree as described by Jeanne de Quillan in *The Gospel of the Beloved Companion: The Complete Gospel of Mary Magdalene,* published by Éditions Athara, 2010.

Guerrand-Hermès Foundation for Peace Research Institute

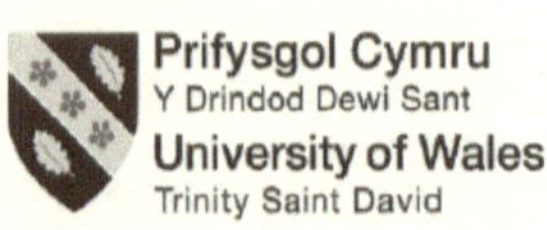

Light, Goodness
Grace, Beauty
Clarity, Truth
Power, Healing
Honour, Humility
Strength, Courage
Love, Compassion
Wisdom, Understanding

Contents

Acknowledgements

In the writing of this book, I have been supported and guided by my colleague Scherto Gill of the Guerrand-Hermès Foundation for Peace as part of our work on A Narrative of Love. The design and layout of the book, based upon the work of Beth Lewis in *Love and the Divine Feminine*, has been undertaken by the graphic designer Lucy Hart of Silverlace Creative. I also want to acknowledge my colleague Lorna Howarth of Panacea Books who undertook the proofreading and guided Lucy and me through the process of publishing on Amazon. Thank you Scherto, Lucy, Lorna and Beth. And I acknowledge the help of Sebastian Betzer and Alex Fiedosiuk who separately researched parts of this text on feminism and relational being for me. Finally, I am most grateful to the Pureland Foundation for their support is making this publication possible.

Introduction

It was the last day of February, 2021, Winter seemed to be easing and on that day my garden was sunlit. There was only the gentlest of breezes. The snowdrops were in full bloom and the daffodils were in bud. There was even the prospect of some easing of the Covid Lockdown. I began to write this book.

Even then I was old, at the end of my seventies, and in the year before, looking around at the growing evidence of possible catastrophe – climate breakdown, pandemics and hate-filled divisiveness – I had published a book called *Love and the Divine Feminine*,[1] in which I asked the questions: how did we get here, and how did we become who we are? I suggested that we are as we are – damaged I fear – because we have lost two great qualities, which as you might guess were Love and the Divine Feminine. I traced the ways in which, for thousands of years, ancient and long-lived cultures intertwined qualities of the feminine and the masculine and expressed them in the form of many goddesses and their consorts, husbands, lovers and sons; and how, almost of a sudden, this was overcome and buried by the worship of warrior gods and then the One God, Yahweh, who alone was supposed to have created the world not through the belly of a woman but through the head of a man. The enormity of this has long since been forgotten.

And then I looked at our more recent history, the last two thousand years in which Jesus, or, as I like to call him, Yeshua, a man whose closest companions and disciples were both women and men, brought us teachings of Love; and I looked at how this loving community was all but dismissed by what became the Great Church, a church dominated by men, the teachings of Love set aside in favour of a doctrine of sin and redemption, founded on crucifixion, resurrection and teachings of original sin, a sin attributed to Eve and thence to all women, not least Mary Magdalene, the companion of Yeshua who fled from Palestine when Yeshua was gone. Out of fear, her role as disciple and teacher was denied by the Great Church, who portrayed her as a repentant prostitute.

And so, at the end of *Love and the Divine Feminine*, I suggested a number of Questions to which, if we would rediscover Love, we should try and find answers. Three of these are the foundation for this book:

1. Can we more explicitly describe principles of Love and if so how might these be applied to the problems that face us today?

2. If there is something that we describe as 'feminine', something that was once regarded as the Divine Feminine, what is it, and what can we say about it? How might this now help us?

3. Is it useful to work with notions of 'the feminine' and 'the masculine' or do these notions create harmful divisions and cloud our understanding? And what would we be able to say about a discourse that was un-gendered, but which spoke of qualities to be found in all of us?

Reflecting on these questions, I realise that whatever I might say about them will be limited by who I am and where I am. I can only respond as an elderly Quaker man living in Suffolk beside the river and the sea. Many of you will have a different insight, and undoubtedly much greater expertise than I have. I can only share my thoughts with you in the hope that they might help, but not replace, your own reflections.

First, in order to say anything at all, I need to say something about the matter of Language, something that has concerned me for many years, and which I have written about again quite recently,[2] for whenever we begin a discourse, begin a conversation or share our writing, we soon discover that our language is at one and the same time powerful and fickle. What we try to share is always shaped by a language that precedes us, a language that we have come to speak but which we have not created for ourselves. It is always a language that has been shaped by others. As the inspirational philosopher, Walter Mignolo, puts it,[3] our language has long since been colonised, and with such effect that many of us are quite unaware that this is so.

But we have to use words as best we can, and I need to use them as I write this text and challenge what we have all been told. For it seems to me that we are presently bound by a language, and by systems and practices, that are no longer suited to the circumstances in which we find ourselves; no longer suited to a world in which we face climate breakdown and resource depletion, no longer suited to a world in which we suffer damaging hostility, prejudice and division. We live in troubled times, and we cannot find our way because we don't know what to say or, perhaps, how to say what we want to say. Fundamental to this condition, to the language we have been given, is an underlying violence towards each other and the Earth that we barely understand – there is a damaging greed and selfishness in us that we have come to take for granted. I want to explore a new and more appropriate language, and a way of being that will enable us to live and flourish in present and likely future times. For until we can imagine another way of being, another discourse, we will remain stranded and mute, unable to comprehend our condition and envision our future.

In all of this, a single principle shapes my work. It is this: that Love is of the Essence.

This book is divided into three parts and ends with some reflections. In the first part, Chapters 1 to 3, which set the scene for what follows, I begin by speaking of the ways in which we are captured by words, and this is followed by an exploration of the meaning of Love and then of Silence. Following on from my book, *Love and the Divine Feminine*, Part Two (Chapters 4 to 6) explores the voices of women, speaking of the divine feminine, of patriarchy, and of feminism, and of the need to find new ways of expressing what we presently call the feminine and the masculine – and of the difficulties of doing this. Although I seek an ungendered discourse, one in which what we sometimes think of as feminine and masculine qualities are shared by both women and men, I believe we have first to restore a proper balance between the masculine and the feminine. And because we have been dominated by men, we must begin by listening to what women have to say. Part Three (Chapters 7 to 10) explores pathways that lead to the possibility of a new language, one that can move us away from where we are towards a future which challenges the presently dominant themes of patriarchy: separation, conflict, greed and selfishness. In this, I start by sharing my readings of other people's work, exploring principles of Partnership, Relational Being and Harmony, and then principles expressed in the ancient Chinese traditions of the I Ching and the Tao. And I complete this part with some thoughts on an Economy of Love and The Practise of Love. At the end of these chapters, in Reflections, I try and draw all of this together by considering what has been said and looking at the questions it raises.

In all of this, I follow a winding path, drawing together in what I can only hope is a way that you can follow, many thoughts and reflections. My style has always been, and is here, somewhat personal. That seems to be the only way I can write, setting words down on the page for you and whoever else may come to read them, as a possible answer to the questions set out above. I hope that you will find some of this at least to be of interest and even, perhaps, of help in your own adventures. I have no doctrine or teaching, only glimpses and intimations garnered whilst walking through the reedbeds and along the footpath that follows the bank of a river.

Endnotes

1. David Cadman, *Love and the Divine Feminine*, Panacea Books, 2020.

2. David Cadman, *A Reflection on Words, Silence and Love*, temenosacademy.org, February 2021.

3. Walter Mignolo, *The Darker Side of the Renaissance: Colonization and the Discontinuity of the Classical Tradition*, Renaissance Quarterly. Vol. 45, No. 4 (Winter, 1992).

Introduction to Part One

The three chapters of Part One provide the setting for all that follows. First, there is a discussion of Language, how it shapes us, sometimes without are knowing, and so how we must pay attention to it. Then, in Chapter 2, comes an exploration of the meaning of Love, as a force that moves mountains, as a matter of virtue, and then as a presence, as being of the essence of all that is. This is followed, in Chapter 3, by a reflection on Silence, its practice, not least amongst Quakers, and most especially its role as the source of Love.

CHAPTER ONE

Language

We start with the matter of Language. When I first wrote about this, some twenty-five years ago, it was in a Temenos Academy paper titled *Lost for Words*,[1] and its premise was that although we are blessed with language, we are also constrained by it. As I said then, whilst the blessings of language are self evident – it is useful, it gives access to the mundane and the practical, it reveals the marvellous and the poetic – the constraints are less obvious, but every bit as real… and much more dangerous.

From our earliest childhood, we are encouraged to put a name to all that we see. As we grow, more names follow, and names not just for those things that we see or touch but, in time, for all that we feel, until, at last, at our peak, if we try, we can even give a name to abstract ideas. Hurrah! Thus, our minds are taught to grasp at our experience and clothe it in words… in language.

However, our language is never entirely our own. It is given to us. It is, and always has been, governed by the base assumptions of those in power, of what they take to be real. In the Middle Ages it would have been popes, bishops and archbishops, perhaps emperors and kings; at the end of the nineteenth century it was industrialists and millowners; and now, of course, it is global corporations, bankers and investment brokers who tell us how we should speak, what we should say. 'Get real', they say. And so our present language, our reality, is set in the framework of competition, markets and prices.

But there is the dilemma. At times, we need to speak of these things, clearly we do, but this 'language of accounting' has outgrown itself and now extends beyond the market place, to define and limit all of our experience. The language of accounting now rules in the hospital ward, the schoolroom and the farm; it rules in local and national government; it governs sports, the theatre and the arts. It is everywhere and governs all.

If you recall the story of The Emperor's New Clothes, you will remember that despite parading himself in what he said were his 'splendid and beautiful new clothes', the emperor was actually naked. But no-one liked to mention it, since they had been told that to do so would make them seem foolish. Just so, there are now things we are not meant to speak of or challenge, and so we don't because to do so would make us seem foolish. But just as what the the emperor claimed to be true was false, so our present language may be less than it appears. For even its masters, those thought to have things firmly in their grasp – bankers and finance directors, treasury officials and, dare it be said, accountants – in truth, oftentimes get it wrong. Anyone who can remember the tales of 'soft landings' and 'the green shoots of recovery', let alone the financial collapse of 2008/9, will know that economies and markets do not always behave as we are told they will; and failures, when they occur, can be spectacular. Despite their image as bastions of financial probity, banks speculate or lend with astonishing imprudence, some even collapse; and more money than most of us can imagine is lost in stock markets that 'unexpectedly' nose-dive; newly-built office buildings, carefully appraised with financial rigour and expertise, remain empty long after they should; and even the priests of this new religion, those most fêted by their peers, are sometimes found to have feet of clay, their proclaimed capacity to turn all to gold proving to be illusory – although you are not supposed to mention it lest you seem foolish.

As a result, we are left with an economy that is so weak that it has to be rescued by subsidy, and an economy requiring that savers earn all but nothing on their savings. I gasp when I recall that in 1996, when I gave that Temenos paper, interest rates on savings accounts were something like 7.5%, and now they are little more than zero; and since 2009, markets have had to be sustained by 'quantitative easing', which is in effect, massive injections of money from the Bank of England (so far something like a trillion pounds). So much for the 'invisible hand' of free markets; so much for the reality that the bankers and accountants speak of.

And yet, of course, we cannot ignore their language, because language has consequences, and whether or not we are aware of it, the domination of their language has come to determine our actions and shape our lives.

This is not news. This is not some radical departure: we have known that this has been so for more than two millennia, for the Buddhist *Dhammapada* opens with this verse:

We are what we think.
All that we are arises with our thoughts.
With our thoughts we make the world.[2]

And again, in another translation:

> What we are today comes from our thoughts of yesterday, and our present thoughts build a life of tomorrow: our life is the creation of our mind.[3]

There it is. We have known it all along. But we haven't paid attention. We haven't insisted it was so. Carelessly perhaps, we have allowed an evidently damaging language to take over our lives, afraid to question it and blinded, it would seem, to its inevitable consequences.

But now we must stop doing this. The crisis is too close. We must open our eyes, see things as they are and then speak of them. For if we wish to understand 'reality', understand who we are and how it is we have come to be as we are, we have to look at *that which we hold to be true*. When all else is stripped away, what is it that defines who we are; and most importantly, what is it that governs our way of being? For with our thoughts we make the world… our life is the creation of our mind.

I suppose it would not be too much of an exaggeration to say that we entered the twenty-first century in the guise of *homo economicus* – that is to say that the characteristics most commonly used to define (perhaps I should say quantify) the nature of our present reality are the characteristics of measurement and in particular the characteristics of costs and revenues. What we have become is a function of this most particular 'language'.[4]

This language, the language that has come to shape our world, has two main characteristics. Firstly, it is reductionistic, which is to say that it is a language of parts and not of wholes. It is a language that encourages us to see ourselves as 'separate from' rather than 'a part of'. And, secondly, as I have said, it is overwhelmingly a language of accounting. It supposes that the things that are real, and of value, are only those that can be measured by price. By contrast, it implies that things that are not readily priced – like Love, for example – are in some sense unreal and therefore of no real value, as though our whole lives could be set within the columns of profit and loss, and all that we are could be captured in the values of a balance sheet.

This language is based upon the proposition that what is

expressed as the real world is confined to that which is tangible, concrete and fixed. Furthermore, it is confined to those things that can be sold and consumed. Nothing else exists, nothing else is of value. And as I have said, the real dilemma is that this language, useful and productive in its own way but nevertheless limited in its relevance, has come to be taken as having universal application. It is applied not simply to some kinds of market transaction, or to our groceries, but to all that we do. It has come to define and limit our experience. It is everywhere and governs all. It has brought us to where we are, which, in truth, is a world of delusion, and if there are benefits in this world, there are certainly costs – a degraded Nature, a broken climate, divisiveness and prejudice in political life, a widening gap between not only the rich and the poor, but between the very rich and everyone else, and above all else an insipient and pervasive violence. Violence and separation are embedded in the language of accounting.

If we would rather be somewhere else – by which I mean a fairer, more just and equitable world, or even, dare I say, a world governed by Love, or at least by compassion and a caring for others and the Earth – then we had best find another language to describe it. But where might we find it?

You will not be surprised to discover that I do not have an answer to this question, but I have long known that one possibility of 'another language' can be found in the *philosophia perennis*, the ancient and eternal wisdom that lies at the root of all of the great spiritual traditions. It is a philosophy that proposes that all arises from a universal metaphysical truth and order.[5] In this realm we cannot define ourselves entirely by reference to the material world since that would be to define us in terms of a part and not a whole. To be whole, we have to be at one with that which is both within and yet beyond the material world, with what we could call the Ultimate Reality, that which, as we shall see, I call Love.

At the same time, since all is one, we cannot separate ourselves entirely from all that is. Rather, we have to practice *being at one* with one another – and this means not only all of humankind but of all beings, all fauna and flora, the mountains and the oceans, the clouds and the winds and the rains. If this all sounds rather familiar, it is because it is – for now, in many ways, the *philosophia perennis* is being spoken of anew by a great multitude, because an increasing number of us are beginning to turn away from what we have always been told is 'just the way things are', to find, most especially in the rising threats of climate change and pandemics, that *we are part of all that is* and, what is more, that we are the source of much of the harm that is caused by the ways in which live.

As we begin to explore the *philosophia perennis* we enter this new realm, moving away from the prosaic to the poetic, from the mundane to the divine, from separation to wholeness, from selfish competition to a more caring collaboration. And it is familiar since this realm already dwells within each one of us and, as if by instinct, some part of us recognises it as being true.

In a Temenos lecture that he gave in London in 2002 to launch his book, *The Wisdom of the Arabs*,[6] my dear friend, the late Professor Suheil Bushrui, talked about the work of Aldous Huxley, who, in 1946, published in London his own collection of sacred texts under the title of *The Perennial Philosophy*.[7] Aldous Huxley, he said, described the realm of the perennial philosophy as a 'divine Reality' of which we are inextricably a part.[8] In this, there was nothing unusual for Aldous Huxley was, after all, restating the teachings of many others before him. But then, with an insight that caused him to be criticised by those who valued the head above the heart, he went on to say something that spoke of how we have to be in order to be able to see these teachings as true; how we need to be in order to hear them. He said:

> But the nature of this one Reality is such that it cannot be directly or immediately apprehended except by those who have chosen to fulfil certain conditions, *making themselves loving, pure in heart, and poor in spirit*. Why should this be so? We do not know. It is just one of those facts which we have to accept, whether we like them or not and however implausible and unlikely they may seem.[9] (My emphasis.)

This apparent heresy of a necessary acceptance should be of interest to us. In a world such as ours that is marked, at least in its public realm, so much by arrogance, control, hatred and violence, this emphasis upon humility and compassion may be of a special importance. And so, given my presumption that we live in an age of delusion, I wonder whether in seeking another language we might attend to Huxley's notion of a Divine Reality. And I also wonder whether, in response to his condition of making ourselves "loving, pure in heart, and poor in spirit," in seeking and following a new path, we may need to discover qualities and practices that are now quite rare, or rather are not taken seriously; the qualities and practise of Love. This aspect, the qualities and practise of Love, will be explored in Chapter 2. But, first, what might this other language of reality be?

As an illustration of a way of being in which we are 'at one', here is a quotation from Huxley's *Perennial Philosophy*. It is from the mediaeval monk Meister Eckhart:

> There is a spirit in the soul, untouched by time and flesh, flowing from the Spirit, remaining in the Spirit, itself wholly spiritual. In this principle is God, ever verdant, ever flowering, in all the joy and glory of His actual Self. Sometimes I have called this principle the Tabernacle of the soul, sometimes a spiritual Light, anon I say it is a Spark. But now I say that it is more exalted above the earth. So I name it in a nobler fashion … It is free of all names and void of all forms. It is one and simple, as God is one and simple, and no man can in any wise behold it.[10]

Something that is "ever verdant, ever flowering" and "free of all names," seems to relate to this problem of naming and holding on to, to which I have already referred.

And then there are two more quotations, this time taken from Professor Bushrui's *The Wisdom of the Arabs*.[11] Again they speak of a oneness with the divine. Both are from one of the earliest Sufi masters, Al-Hallaj:

> Thou art my life and the innermost secret of my heart;
> Wherever I am, there also art thou…[12]

I am He whom I love and He whom I love is I;
We are two souls dwelling in one body.
When you look at me you can see Him,
And you can see us both when you look at Him.[13]

Two souls dwelling in one body, and "when you look at me you can see Him." Utter unity. Is this a guide? Is there something in the notion of oneness rather than separation that gives us a direction?

Even if we do not use the language of a personal God, a Him to whom we can turn – and not everyone does – these quotations provide us with a very different idea of who we are. For if we really do take ourselves to be defined only as, and limited by, *homo economics*, then the rules of the marketplace and the balance of accounts set the parameters of our reason and of our being. We must be subservient to the algebra and algorithms of pricing. In the end, quite literally, it is markets and the economy that matter. However, if, perhaps in some mysterious way that we cannot explain, we see ourselves as unified with, and as an expression of, that which we might call 'divine', that which is within and beyond us, then reverence for others now present or yet to come must cause us to temper our own desires and actions with those qualities that are the teaching of all the great spiritual traditions – generosity, patience, simplicity, humility, harmlessness, compassion and so on, the very qualities that Aldous Huxley thought were necessary for those who would be able to understand and to practice the perennial philosophy, those that he referred to as being loving, pure in heart, and poor in spirit.

This begins to hold together, and the more I think about it, and even if I struggle with the form of the words – and I do – the more it seems to me that it is beyond doubt that the choices we make about 'language' and 'reality' will always, and inevitably, lead us in particular directions. There are always consequences.

Again, this is not a new idea. Those of you who are familiar with Buddhist texts will know the prophetic story of the wheel-turning king who failed to give to the poor. Poverty lead to theft, theft to violence and so on and so on until at the lowest point, at the depth of degradation, just a few people had the insight and courage to turn away from the seemingly unstoppable tragedy and, once more, proclaim the ancient wisdom of generosity, simplicity and compassion until, as again one thing led to another, the wellbeing of all was restored.[14] Will there now be, I wonder, those who have the insight and courage to prick the bubble of our delusion, tell us that the emperor has no clothes on, and help us to see how we may prevent or at least live with the myriad crises that are looming? We must pray that this is so, otherwise we may discover that those who profess calamity are prophetic, for, unchecked, the language of accounting will continue to promote its own dangerous and damaging fantasy, promising ever-increasing consumption for all, and thereby reinforcing the environmental and social catastrophes that have already begun to wreak havoc.

Since giving that Temenos paper twenty-five years ago, I have come to see that language is not only a constraint, and sometimes a damaging constraint, but also that we often struggle to find truth in words or texts alone. Texts, prosaic texts – for poetry I think is another matter – seem to be riven with partiality, uncertainty and, to some extent, unreliability and misleading bias, very often marked by the particular circumstances of their time and place. It is as if there is no common or adequate vocabulary or discourse.

But there is a dilemma. Words may fail us, but what then shall we do? How do we challenge a dominant and evidently damaging and unjust language? To be heard, we seem to have to speak of it whilst using the very language we decry. Again and again, I have come across the difficulty of finding 'agreeable' words; again and again I have been told that nothing can be done unless what is proposed fits into, or is spoken of, in 'acceptable' terms – to fit into the language of business and economy – even though we now know beyond doubt that this language only brings us back to where we are. Even now, after years of discussion about sustainability, corporate responsibility, responsible investment and the costs of environmental and social degradation, we seem to be stranded in the place that this language has led us to. And despite the very many places where this is challenged, it would seem that we cannot move beyond it.

But we can no longer remain where we are if we are to avoid significant calamity. We must find 'another language', and another way of being. For as we speak, so we are. Here are words of the late Philip Sherrard:

[How] we perceive things depends crucially upon the state of our consciousness, and…the state of our consciousness depends on the state of our being. This does not mean that the reality of things themselves varies according to the consciousness which perceives them, and still less that their existence is dependent upon their being perceived. It simply means that how they appear to us, *the kind of reality we attribute to them*, and whether we see them as they are or, as it were, through a distorting lens, have very little to do with the things themselves and very much to do with the quality of our own being, the purity of our soul and the level of our intelligence. And this in turn means that the way in which we see things *may not correspond in the least to the reality of the things themselves.*[15] (My emphases.)

It is increasingly understood, not least in science and ecology, that if we are to see things as they really are we must see them not as fixed, independent and separate but as ever-changing, connected and whole; that all that is, is part of an intricate web of being, a web of causation and dependency, a web of relationships; and that we should see ourselves as 'a part of' and not 'apart from'. Indeed, perhaps the most compelling idea of our time is the rediscovery of what we might call *a reality of relatedness* – to which I will turn in Chapter 7. In physics, in biology, in economics, in medicine, in the arising of the entire debate about 'sustainability' and what might be termed the environmental or ecological crisis, the limits of reductionism and a science of parts are being exposed as false, and a new reality of connectedness and wholeness is emerging. Furthermore, it is understood that these relationships are essentially dynamic. Far from being fixed and certain, reality is characterised by fluidity, by shift and change. Indeed, our reality of *relatedness* is, in truth, a reality of *relatingness*, that it to say that it can only be realised by being experienced. It is a reality that requires not disinterested observation but mindful participation.

This vision of a world of constantly shifting relationships, coming to be and ceasing to be, is not, of course, in the least bit new. The ancient Greek, Heraclitus, for example, saw reality as an ever-changing river where 'everything flows'; and such a reality also lies at the heart of the Buddhist notions of impermanence and emptiness,[16] which are the foundation of the Four Noble Truths.[17] For at the very moment of his awakening, the Buddha spoke of arising and ceasing, of the knowledge of "the passing away and reappearance of things."[18]

More especially, this reality of relatingness is expressed in the Buddhist teaching of *paticca samuppda* or 'dependent origination' – that there are no absolutes but only a shifting pattern of interacting connections:

> That is when this is; that arises with the arising of this. That is not when this is not; that ceases with the cessation of this.[19]

Here, the phenomenon of arising and ceasing would seem to be extended beyond mere linear causality to include a much more radical *reciprocity*, which, again, lies at the very heart of the teachings of the Buddha. For it is taught:

> One who sees *paticca samuppāda* sees the Dhamma; one who sees the Dhamma sees *paticca samuppāda*.[20]

But what lies behind this understanding of causality and the web of being? Where does it lead us? Is there some further destination or is this all that there is – arising and ceasing?

This is a question that brings us to the next matter, the matter of Love: what is it and how can we find our way towards it?

Endnotes

1. A version of this paper was included within a paper written for the Temenos Academy in 2021 and reproduced on their website temenosacademy.org.

2. *The Dhammapada*, a new rendering by Thomas Byrom, Vintage Books, New `York, 1976, 3.

3. *The Dhammapada*, translated by Juan Mascro, Penguin Books, England, 1973, 35.

4. The following two paragraphs are largely taken from: David Cadman, 'With Our Thoughts We Make the World', *A Sacred Trust*, The Temenos Academy and The Prince's Foundation, 2002, 163-4.

5. The Temenos Academy (temenosacademy.org) runs a two-year Foundation Course in the Perennial Philosophy, which they described as being "like an underground river, [which] has flowed through all civilizations and all ages, and wherever it sends up springs and fountains, Beauty and Wisdom have flowered."

6. Suheil Bushrui, *The Wisdom of the Arabs*, Oneworld, Oxford, 2002.

7. Aldous Huxley, *The Perennial Philosophy* Chatto and Windus, London, 1946. Gottfried Leibniz is thought to have first coined the phrase *philosophia perennis* some three hundred years ago and many other writers, not least traditionalists such as René Guénon, Frithjof Schuon and K. A . Coomaraswamy, have also spoken of these eternal truth. Both Guénon and Coomaraswamy are referred to by Huxley.

8.   Ibid. 1972 edition. 1.

9.   Ibid. 2-3.

10.   Ibid. 22-23.

11.   Op cit, Suheil Bushrui.

12.   Ibid. 29.

13.   Ibid. 31.

14.   Dígha Nikáya, Division 111.26.

15.   *A Sacred Trust: Ecology and Spiritual Vision*, edited by David Cadman and John Carey, The Temenos Academy, 2002, 2.

16.   In Pali, impermanence and emptiness are known as *aniccat* and *sunyata*.

17.   *Majjhima Nikaya*, (MN) Tr. by Bhikkhu Nanamoli and Bhikkhu Bodhi Sutta 9, 132-144.

18.   Ibid. Sutta 4.29, 105.

19.   Ibid. Note 408, 1231-2.

20.   Ibid. Sutta 28.28, 283.

CHAPTER TWO

Love's Meaning

So much has been written and said about Love, that whatever I have to say will be the tiniest crumb upon the table. However, this is a matter to which I have turned many times, and I have a proposition: that Love matters. As I said in the Introduction to *Love and the Divine Feminine*:

> There is a Presence, a form of Being which is beyond our understanding. It is Good and it is Loving. When we surrender to it, we are loved by it and we are drawn to love it. Given the limitations of our knowing, we begin to endow this Presence with personality, for that is what we find in ourselves. And then, for comfort, we call it God. But the moment we do so, the moment we seek to name it, we begin to limit it, to make it less than it is. And then we limit it again and call it Father, excluding half of our nature, and if we are not careful, we place Him far away, in the sky above us and wonder how we shall ever reach Him.
>
> Love is not man or woman. Love is Divine Presence, and this Presence is the energetic force that shapes all relationships when they are most natural and at their best. Love is the primal impulse, and it is no *thing*, but rather a *movement* from and towards. We have to *be* in Love. This is the truth that lies behind the Christian commandment to 'love God' and to 'love one another', and to keep this commandment we have to *be in Love*.
>
> Just suppose that we are being called to a new Gospel of Love in which there is a marriage between the Divine Feminine and the Divine Masculine, an integration, a new consciousness. I think that this is possible, and that it is required.[1]

Looking back, I see that there have been two vital influences that have shaped my life and brought me to this place. The first is a birthright of Quakerism with its parables and the words of the man I like to call Yeshua. The second, and later, is the teaching of the

Buddha. I understand those who say that you must choose a path and stick to it, but in my case these two paths have become intertwined like a honeysuckle and a rose. The rose is my birthright and was in place before the teachings of the Buddha grew upon it. Now their fragrance has become one. For they share, as it were, a common root, a root that is grounded in teachings of love and compassion.

Because a sense of the sacred has been so much removed from our lives, from our language, the very word 'Love' has been diminished; has, perhaps, come to mean little more than personal desire, affection, even sentimentality, or worse still a narrow virtue. None of these will do. Love is something much more profound than this. It is *of the nature of true being*. It is elemental. It is that which is captured in the Arabic word *Mahabbah*, which means Love as the underlying principle of the universe;[2] it is that which the late Sir John Templeton referred to as "Ultimate Reality";[3] it is the very "breath of the Divinity"[4] and, as such, it is the ground of kindness, reciprocity and relatingness. It is that which the Orthodox Philip Sherrard called the "irreducible touchstone" of life, an "ontological tenderness:"

> Only in and through love is the innermost reality of things disclosed and fulfilled. Such love is not a divine quality, still less is it a personal attribute, something merely human and emotional. Apart from love there is no reason for the existence of the world – 'God so loved the world' – and apart from love the world has no purpose in existing, all other purposes being either auxiliary or merely false and superfluous. It is the irreducible touchstone; it is the seal and the consummation of the sacred.[5]

This Love lies at the very heart of Buddhism where it is expressed in the teaching of the unity of wisdom and compassion. Indeed, in one of the earliest texts[6] it is said that it is only by dwelling in the realm of the four divine abodes[7] of loving kindness, compassion, appreciative joy[8] and equanimity that enlightenment is to be found. And at the heart of my Quaker childhood, with its emphasis upon silent contemplation, non-violence and tolerance, there was a teaching that stressed the strength and gentleness of Yeshua as the good shepherd – his compassion for the suffering of others, and his assurance that those who would find the kingdom of heaven would not be the rich and the powerful but the meek, the merciful, and the pure in heart. I was brought up to believe in turning the other cheek, going the extra mile, the parable of the Good Samaritan. Yeshua was a man who taught kindliness and selflessness for everyone, and who encapsulated the core of his teaching in the following words:

> A new commandment I give unto you, That ye love one another; as I have loved you, that ye also love one another.[9]

Now, many years later, it seems to me, that this teaching is even more profound than I had supposed. Not only are we being taught that we should love one another as a matter of virtue, we are, I believe, being taught that love, or rather Love, is *of the essence*. For it is also said:

> We are of God… for love is of God…God is love; and he that dwelleth in love dwelleth in God, and God in him…because as he is, so are we in this world. [10]

And if all that is comes from this 'God', then God is in all that is. And if God is Love, then, surely, what we are being told is that all that is is Love – all of us, all of life, the rose and the honeysuckle, the coming and going of the seasons, the wind, the sun and the rain, the in-breath and the out-breath.

As the American scholar Whitall N. Perry puts it in his *Treasury of Traditional Wisdom*:

> Love is the energizing elixir of the universe, the cause and effect of all harmonies, light's brilliance and the heat in wine and fire, it is the aroma of perfumes and the breath of the Divinity: it is the Life in all being…It is all that the texts have to say, and the more that remains unspoken.[11]

It is that which the Christian mystic Julian of Norwich refers to as "our Lord's meaning."

Love's Meaning

From time to time these things were first revealed. I had often wanted to know what was our Lord's meaning. It was more than fifteen years after that I was answered in my spirit's understanding. 'You would know our Lord's meaning in this thing? Know it well. Love was his meaning. Who showed it you? Love. What did he show you? Love. Why did he show it? For love. Hold on to this and you will know and understand love more and more. But you will not know or learn anything else – ever!' So it was that I learned that love was our Lord's meaning.[12]

In all of this, then, is there not a suggestion that the natural state of the world, its essence, is the very manifestation of Love; that love is in all or is expressed in all; that the fragrance of both the Great Reality, and the reality of our everyday lives, is divine order and harmony? Surely, this must be the 'divine Reality' of the perennial philosophy. And if this is so, then it must shape all that we do.

In an age that so often favours the head against the heart, it is worth noting that in both the Christian and the Buddhist traditions the Way of Love, the way of compassion, is not described by reference to some complex theoretical proposition. Indeed, in Buddhism, the story of the poisoned arrow,[13] quite specifically advises against such speculation. Rather, in both traditions, Love is taught by reference to everyday practise. Again and again in the teachings and parables of Yeshua we are presented with practical acts of selflessness and gentleness that reveal a common ground of love and compassion – the Good Samaritan, the forgiveness of the prodigal son, the anointing of the feet of Yeshua by Mary Magdalene, "that ye love one another."

And in Paul the Apostle's First Letter to the Corinthians[14] we are given the very characteristics of what it is to be loving. The text is so especially beautiful that I cannot resist quoting it:

Love suffereth long, and is kind; love envieth not; love vaunteth not itself, is not puffed up,
Doth not behave itself unseemly, seeketh not her own, is not easily provoked, thinketh no evil;
Rejoiceth not in iniquity, but rejoiceth in the truth;
Beareth all things, believeth all things, hopeth all things, endureth all things.
Love never faileth…

In an essay entitled 'The Greatest Thing in the World',[15] the Scottish evangelist, Henry Drummond, analysed these characteristics to provide A Spectrum of Love, which had nine ingredients. They are:

Patience	"Love suffereth long."
Kindness	"And is kind."
Generosity	"Love envieth not."
Humility	"Love vaunteth not itself, is not puffed up."
Courtesy	"Does not behave itself unseemly."
Unselfishness	"Seeketh not her own."
Good Temper	"Is not easily provoked."
Guilelessness	"Thinketh no evil."
Sincerity	"Rejoiceth not in iniquity, but rejoiceth in the truth."

"You will observe," he said, that all of these characteristics are "in relation to life, in relation to the known to-day and the near to-morrow, and not to the unknown eternity." [16]

Interestingly but not, of course, surprisingly, the four divine abodes of Buddhism[17] are also said to lead to a set of 'perfections' that bear a strong similarity to Paul's characteristics of Love. The Ten Perfections, or *paramitas*, are:[18]

Generosity, Morality, Renunciation, Wisdom, Energy, Patience, Truthfulness, Resolution, Loving-kindness and Equanimity.

And, indeed, it is these qualities that are expressed in the Buddha's teaching on loving-kindness, the *Metta Sutta*, where, for example we are urged to be straightforward and gentle in speech, be at ease and frugal in our ways, not to be angry or harm one another, cherishing all living beings and radiating kindness, free of hatred, pure hearted and with clarity of vision.[19]

Then, quite recently, I received from my friend, Bob Boisture, who is the President and CEO of the Fetzer Institute in America, the following statement of the Institute's Ten Affirmations of the Meaning of Love:[20]

1. Love is at the heart of the Sacred Mystery we call Spirit.
2. Love is relational. It leads us to embrace our relatedness to Sacred Mystery and the Cosmos, which encompasses the Earth and the community of life it supports, including all persons and society.
3. Love is generous. It endlessly gives itself away, dynamically and creatively embracing all.
4. Love desires communion with the beloved and the flourishing of the beloved.
5. Love, present at our beginning, accompanies each step on our life's journey and is our true destination.
6. Love invites, animates, and empowers human love, the highest expression of our freedom. Human love cannot be coerced. Love calls and helps us to labor freely to unfold our full human potentials for shared flourishing.
7. Love calls forth and deepens our commitment to truth. Moreover, there is "heart-knowing" that complements other valuable modes of knowing.
8. Love animates justice. It calls us to give freely and gladly what is due to the whole community of life, including other persons and society. Love summons us, despite danger and discomfort, to labor shoulder-to-shoulder with those denied justice. It asks us to transform our hearts and unjust social structures and to unmask and resist all forms of scapegoating and oppression.
9. Love heals. It empowers us to open ourselves to healing,

help others mend, re-knit torn societies, and transform
and heal cultural memories. Love can give us the personal
and collective courage for deepening honesty, repentance,
restitution, forgiveness, reconciliation, and joyous community.
10. Love calls us to radically re-imagine our lives, societies, and
ways of dwelling on Earth. It calls us all to solidarity in Love,
rooted in our plural experiences of Sacred Mystery, for the
shared flourishing of the community of being.

It is encouraging that an organisation such as the Fetzer
Institute is speaking out on these matters, insisting on Love against
all the obstacles, and despite those who doubt Love's meaning. And
for Fetzer, this over-riding aim is expressed as building a spiritual
foundation for a loving world.[21]

Thus, it would seem that in both Christianity and Buddhism,
this Love, this root cause, this organising principle, this essence, is to
be discovered not in elaborate theory but in the everyday, and in the
practise of small things: harmlessness, patience, generosity, kindness,
humility. It is in places such as this that we find the entangled
fragrance of the honeysuckle and the rose.

But if these two traditions, Quaker and Buddhist, have been the
ground of my being, or rather, Being, there are other teachings that
whilst less familiar to me seem to have much that is common, eternal
and universal.

For example, another expression of Love as being of the essence,
of being the organising principle of the world, is provided in the
Orthodox teaching of the Trinity. In his book *The Orthodox Way*,[22]
published in 1998, Bishop Kallistos Ware, as he then was, described
the nature of the relationship between the Father and the Son as a
relationship of mutual love – the Father for the Son and the Son for
the Father:

To speak in this way of God as Son and Father is at once to imply a movement of mutual love…It is to imply that from all eternity God himself, as Son, in filial obedience and love renders back to God the Father the being which the Father by paternal self-giving eternally generates in him.[23]

I do not speak of God as a Father with a Son, but I accept that what Bishop Kallistos Ware was saying is in accordance with a tradition in whose presence I have felt that which is Holy. Standing in the church of the Monastery of Vatopedi on Mount Athos, caught within the liturgical chanting of the monks, the light of the candles of the corona and the circling smoke of the incense, that Other, for which there really is no name, is so intense as to be almost tangible.

And then, of course, in the Sufi tradition of Islam, we find a quite extraordinary and ecstatic expression of Love. Indeed, we might say that there is no tradition in which Love is more intensively expressed. We find, for example, the poet Rumi drenched in love for the beloved:

> A lifetime without Love is of no account
> Love is the Water of Life
> Drink it down with heart and soul.[24]

And Love like a great force is everywhere:

> Love makes the sea boil like a cauldron,
> Love reduces the mountains to sand.
> Love cracks hundreds of fissures into the heavens unconsciously,
> Love makes the earth tremble.
> …(God said): "If it wasn't by pure love, how could I have
>   brought the heavens into existence?
> I have elevated the sublime celestial sphere so that you could
>   understand the sublimity of Love."[25]

The more that I have explored this remarkable expression of Love, the more humble I have felt, and the less I have felt I should say. This is the fragrance of the most delightful and entrancing of blossoms, an exotic perfume, something quite beyond my experience of the honeysuckle and the rose. With my Quaker childhood and its teaching of reserve and moderation, such ecstasy probably lies beyond me. I fear that I shall never quite be able to find in myself that quality of abandonment that it requires, never, perhaps, be able to find these Gardens of Paradise. This is my loss.

By contrast, a more calming fragrance, and one in which I have found great comfort, is offered by the devout expressions of Love of the Brahma Kumaris.[26] The Brahma Kumaris teach a form of Raja Yoga, a meditation practice that presents the true self as soul, an eternal being at peace and full of Love. The divine, they say, can be experienced as an ocean of Love that brings tranquillity and understanding, a deep sense of peace and wellbeing that enables us to see the world more clearly, and engage with it more effectively. A central part of this teaching is that both the soul and the divine are to be experienced as a point of light – infinite and eternal. In meditation the body and its senses are seen as being no more than a garment worn by the eternal soul, a tool with which the soul can engage with the mundane world.

The inspiration of the Brahma Kumaris is *The Bhagavad Gita*, a text of such wisdom and beauty that one stands before it in awe and astonishment. It is redolent with the immanence of the divine and the fragrance of Love:

I am the taste of living waters [says Krishna] and the light of the sun and the moon. I am OM, the sacred word of the Vedas, sound in silence, heroism in men.

I am the pure fragrance that comes from the earth and the brightness of fire. I am the life of all living beings, and the austere life of those who train their souls.[27]

He who in this oneness of love, loves me in whatever he sees, wherever this man may live, in truth this man lives in me.[28]

Only by love can men see me, and know me, and come unto me.[29]

At one point in the *Gita*, Arjuna asks the Lord Krishna to tell him "who are the best Yogis?" Krishna replies with a great list of qualities that are dear to him, but in the end he says:

...even dearer to me are those who have faith and love...[30]

The delight of the teaching of the Brahma Kumaris is that they open the gateway to the Garden of the Soul, a place of such peace and tranquillity that all else is as nothing. This is the place of unconditional love, quite literally Being *in* Love. And to find it, they say, you simply have to be who you truly are. It is always there whether you find your way to it or not. It is there as you breath in and as you breathe out. It never fails since it always is. Like the incense of the church in Vatopedi, it is a 'fragrance' that cannot be captured in words but only in experience, and it is not about knowing but about being. The question, then, would seem to be not 'What shall we do?' but 'How shall we be?', that is, 'How shall we Be with the divine?'[31]

In all that I have described so far, with all its apparent diversity of expression, it is clear that there are perhaps two particular ways of speaking of Love. The first can be termed as *elemental* – that Love is the Ultimate Reality or that it is a great force that Rumi says makes "the earth tremble" or makes "the sea boil like a cauldron." The second is that it is *personal and social*, that it is expressed in our relationships with one another and with all that is – it is patient, peaceful, kind and compassionate, it is wise and truthful. So much is known of this, and so much has already been set down in texts or in images that if we fail to practise it, it cannot be for the lack of telling, but only because we choose to disregard it. We have known that it is true for a very long time, but now the difference is that, above all else, we must attend to it with urgency.

In the Preface to *Love and the Divine Feminine*, Love speaks and says:

> "I am the messenger of stars, and of river, wind and earth. Hear me. Invite me in, and for a while suppose what I say is true." [32]

What might happen if we were to suppose that what Love says is true?

I come to an end of this chapter, with this quotation from one of the earliest Quakers, William Penn, who, speaking in 1693, but with words that are as relevant today as they were then, said this:

> A good end cannot sanctify evil means; nor must we ever do evil, that good may come of it … We are too ready to retaliate, rather than forgive, or gain by love and information. And yet we could hurt no man that we believe loves us. Let us then try what love will do: for if men did once see we love them, we should soon find they would not harm us. Force may subdue, but love gains: and he that forgives first, wins the laurel. [33]

Perhaps then, in seeking a new pathway, in trying to discover a new language, we might "try what love will do".

Endnotes

1. David Cadman, *Love and the Divine Feminine*, Panacea Books, 2020, 12.

2. I am most grateful to my dear friend, the late Professor Suheil Bushrui, for pointing this out to me. The word is part of the teaching of the Bahá'ís.

3. Stephen G. Post, *Is Ultimate Reality Unlimited Love?*, Templeton Press, 2014.

4. See below, Whitall N. Perry.

5. *Temenos Academy Review*, Volume 9, 1998, 234.

6. Op cit, MN Sutta 52, the *Atthakanāgara Suuta*.

7. In Pali, the four divine abodes are the *brahma-vihara*, which are *mettā* (loving kindness), *karunā*, (compassion), *muditā* (appreciative joy) and *upekkhā* (equanimity).

8. This is sometimes termed 'joy in and for others'.

9. Gospel of St. John, Chapter 13, v. 34.

10. I John, 4, v.v. 6-17.

11. Whitall N. Perry, *A Treasury of Traditional Wisdom*, Fons Vitae, 2000, 612.

12. Quoted in Dorothea Siegmund-Schultze, 'Some Aspects of Julian of Norwich's *Revelations of Divine Love*,' 199-210.

13. The Cula-Malunkyovada Sutta: The Shorter Instructions to Malunkya (MN 63), translated from the Pali by Thanissaro Bhikkhu, Access to Insight, 14 June 2010.

14. I Corinthians, Chapter 13.

15. Henry Drummond, 'The Greatest Thing in the World,' *The Compact Treasury of Inspiration*, Edited by Kenneth S Giniger, Festival Books Ser., Nashville, TN, USA: Abingdon Press, 1977, 242 *et seq*.

16. Ibid.

17. MN Sutta 52, the *Atthakanāgara Suuta*, described above.

18. Nyanatiloka, Buddhist Dictionary, 1997, 147-8. The Pali equivalent words are: *dāna-pārami, sîla-pārami, nekkhamma-p, pannā-p, viriya-p, khanti-p, sacca-p, adhitthana-p, mettā-p* and *upekkhā-p*.

19. This comes from a translation of the *Metta Sutta*, itself a part of the *Sutta Nipāta*, is from Sharon Salzberg, *Loving Kindness*, Shambhala, Boston & London, 1995.

20. Drawing heavily on the wisdom of the world's faith traditions, the Fetzer Institute Board of Trustees developed these Affirmations to guide our work in helping to build the spiritual foundation for a loving world.

21. fetzer.org

22. Bishop Kallistos Ware, *The Orthodox Way*, St Vladimir's Seminary Press, 1998.

23. Ibid, 32.

24.   Divan-i-Shams, 11909.

25.   *Mathnawi*, v. 2375.

26.   The Brahma Kumaris were founded in what is now Pakistan
       in 1936 by a remarkable man, Brahma Baba, who dedicated
       the rest of his long life to bringing into reality a vision of
       people of all cultural, economic and religious backgrounds
       coming together to rediscover and develop the spiritual
       dimension of their lives. In 1951, he founded a university on
       Mount Abu in Rajasthan; today that university has grown,
       and his movement has extended worldwide with around
       3,500 branches in 70 countries. Their teaching is a form of
       Raja Yoga.

27.   *The Bhagavad Gita*, Penguin Classics, 1962, 36. 7.8 and
       7.9.

28.   Ibid, 34. 6.31.

29.   Ibid, 58. 11.54.

30.   Ibid, 61.

31.   This teaching was given to me by the late Dadi Janki, then
       co-leader of the Brahma Kumaris.

32.   Op cit, David Cadman, 6.

33.   William Penn, *Some Fruits of Solitude*, 1693 maxims 537,
       543-546 quoted in *Quaker Faith and Practice* 24.03.

CHAPTER THREE

And Then There Was Silence...

Finally, as part of this beginning, I wish to take us into Silence. For the practice of mindfulness and contemplation as a source of Love is an essential part, indeed the ground, of all and each of the diverse and different teachings of which I have spoken. It lies, of course, at the root of Quakerism and of Buddhism, but it is also to be found in Christian Orthodoxy, Sufism and Raja Yoga.

For Quakers, silent contemplation, prayer and worship is said to lead us to the still centre of our being. In our Quaker meetings, we hold the silence and the silence holds us. When we step *into* it, we are refreshed by it, comforted by it, inspired by it, and while we remain there, and even when we have left it behind for another day, we are drawn to serve it. In deep unity with others, this is a place in which we discover our relationships and find an awareness of our true reality. It is a place where we wait on the divine, a place that is very much like the one described by T. S. Eliot in *East Coker*:

> I said to my soul, be still, and wait without hope
> For hope would be hope for the wrong thing; wait without love
> For love would be love of the wrong thing; there is yet faith
> But the faith and the love and the hope are all in the waiting.
> Wait without thought, for you are not ready for thought;
> So the darkness shall be the light, and the stillness the dancing.
> Whisper of running streams, and winter lightning.
> The wild thyme unseen and the wild strawberry.[1]

Not only do silence, prayer and reflection form the core of Quaker worship, they are also part of daily life. For example, Quaker business meetings begin and end with a period of silence, and it is to silence that we return for guidance in times of difficulty, despair or dispute.

In Buddhism, mindfulness is part of the teaching of the Eightfold Path that leads to the cessation of suffering.[2] Here, too, the practice of meditation leads to a state of attentive tranquillity in

And Then There Was Silence…

which, letting go of the distracting restlessness of our mind, we come
to see things as they are – that there is suffering, impermanence and
emptiness. In this state we open our hearts to both wisdom and
compassion. Abiding in Love we find insight.

Silent prayer and contemplation are present also in the hesychast
tradition of Orthodoxy where, as Sherrard tells us:

> …it is only through the contemplative life in all its aspects…that
> we can actualize in ourselves the personal love and knowledge of
> God on which depend not only our own authentic existence as
> human beings, but also our capacity to cooperate with God in
> fulfilling the innermost purposes of creation.[3]

And it is there in the Sufi tradition of Islam. Indeed, in discussing
the poetry of Rumi, the scholar Annemarie Schimmel says:

> Becoming silent, because the secret of Love cannot be conveyed
> … is a motif which occurs often in his early poems. The word
> *khāmush*, "silent," "quiet," is used so frequently that some scholars
> have been inclined to regard it as being Rumi's original nom de
> plume.[4]

The Raja Yoga of the Brahma Kumaris is essentially a yoga of
mindfulness and silent contemplation, and in the *Gita* it is said:

> When a man dwells in the solitude of silence, and meditation
> and contemplation are ever with him; when too much food does
> not disturb his health, and his thoughts and words and body are
> in peace; when freedom from passion his constant will;
> And his selfishness and violence and pride are gone; when
> lust and anger and greediness are no more, and he is free from the
> thought 'this is mine'; then this man has risen on the mountain
> of the Highest: he is worthy to be one with Brahman, with God.
>
> He is one with Brahman, with God, and beyond grief and
> desire his soul is in peace. His love is one for all creation, and he
> has supreme love for me.

By love he knows me in truth, who I am and what I am. And when he knows me in truth he enters into my Being.[5]

And, more recently, I have found it expressed in a wonderful passage of the *Gospel of Mary Magdalene*. The version I like to read is the one written by Jean-Yves Leloup and translated into English by Joseph Rowe.[6] Towards the end of the gospel, Mary Magdalene is speaking of a recent teaching she has received from her Teacher, Yeshua:

'Henceforth I travel towards Repose
where time rests in the Eternity of Time;
I go now into Silence.'
Having said all this, Mary became silent,
for it was in silence that the Teacher spoke to her.

This is such a beautiful and intriguing text, since not only does Mary choose Silence, but she also refers to having been taught in silence. In his commentary on this passage, Jean-Yves Leloup says that the place of Repose, the place to which Mary is travelling, is a place beyond ordinary time, a place where there is nothing for the senses to grasp on to. It is a place which lacks all sensations, emotions and thoughts. *There is only Silence.* Even love does not feel like love in this space. Not as we know it. And yet it is there that we find the very source of Love.

It seems to me, then, that each of these teachings, separately and together, tell us that the ground of reality, or Reality, the still point of being and Being, is to be found in contemplation and meditation; that such reflection, such practice, is the *necessary foundation* of true action, and that this is also the source of Love; it is where Love dwells – it is there all the time, waiting for us.

This being so, we need profoundly to change our perspective, our ways of being. Returning to the proposition put forward in Chapter 1, that we need to find a new language, to move away from an ethos of separation, conflict and competition towards one of wholeness, co-operation and compassion, I note that in his introduction to the poetry of Rumi, Colman Barks says that all language "is a longing

And Then There Was Silence…

for home."[7] All language, especially all naming and numbering and the work of the rational mind, is a struggling attempt to regain and give expression to that which has been lost. And that which has been lost is a sense of one-ness, of being at one with, of Being in (within) Love.

But we do not always need to name our paths or even try to describe them. Rather, we need to walk along them, shuffle about and sit by the roadside, meeting companions, sharing food and stories. Naming them is just words, and in the end they fail us, for as we have seen, Love is beyond anything that we can say. Indeed, the irony is that in the end, in an age that is full of noise and distraction, we come once again to Stillness and Silence, the dwelling place of the divine.

In *Quaker Faith and Practice* it is said:

> So one approaches, by efforts which call for the deepest resources of one's being, to the condition of true silence; not just of sitting still, not just of not speaking, but of a wide awake, fully aware non-thinking. It is in this condition, found and held for a brief instant only, that I have experienced the existence of something other than 'myself'. The thinking me has vanished, and with it vanishes the sense of separation, of unique identity. One is not left naked and defenceless… One becomes instead aware, one is conscious of being a participant in the whole of existence, not limited to the body or the moment… It is in this condition that one understands the nature of the divine power, its essential identity with love, in the widest sense of that much misused word.[8]

In the words of the Buddha:

> When a man knows the solitude of silence, and feels the joy of quietness, he…feels the joy of the DHAMMA.[9]

In the words of the *Gita*:

When the sage of silence…closes the doors of his soul and, resting his inner gaze between the eyebrows, keeps peaceful and even the ebbing and flowing of breath; and with life and mind and reason in harmony, and with desire and fear and wrath gone, keeps silent his soul before final freedom, he in truth has attained final freedom.[10]

And for Rumi, too, in the end there is only silence:

When it comes to Love, I have to be silent…
To describe Love, intellect is like an ass is a morass,
The pen breaks when it is to describe Love.[11]

So be it.

Somewhat oddly then, it seems to me that the starting point of a journey towards Love is not political activism or even social conscience. Nor is it intellectual endeavour, the writing of books and the giving of lectures. Rather, I suggest, and Covid has now surely made this clear, that it is the rare qualities of *slowness* and an *attentive* and *compassionate silence* which, when practised together and with intent, lead us towards a necessary path of Love. It may be difficult for us in the West and in the twenty-first century to accept that slowness might add to our well-being and that silence and compassion might bring happiness. But that, of course, is the teaching of the sacred tradition of wholeness, of holiness – that to become whole, to be fully ourselves and at one with all that is, we have to learn to dwell in the divine.

Such a dwelling requires a certain spontaneity and a vivacity of spirit, but above all else it also requires an uncommon capacity for slowness. Like many of us, I suspect, for most of my life I have had an obsession with 'doing', seldom living in the present, but always in some kind of anxious future. But I have come to see this as a mighty hindrance – although I have to admit that I still have great difficulty changing my ways of being and putting this lesson into practice!

So far, I have quoted from unquestionably profound sources such as the *Dhammapada*, Meister Eckhart and Al-Hallaj. By contrast, some years ago I read the following extract from the *Curly Pyjama*

And Then There Was Silence…

Letters[12] on the noticeboard at Schumacher College in England:

> Dear Vasco, in response to your question "what is worth doing and what is worth having?" I would like to say this. It is worth doing nothing and having a rest; in spite of all the difficulty it may cause, you must rest Vasco – otherwise you will become RESTLESS! I believe the world is sick with exhaustion and dying of restlessness… Yours sleepily, Mr. Curly

At once, I hear the outraged voices of those who see that there is much to be done and who, like me, carry the childhood burden of always having to have something to do. But on reflection, is not Mr. Curly right when he goes on to point out that our restlessness and consequent fatigue are "ultimately soul destroying as well as earth destroying"?

The Buddha regarded restlessness as one of the Five Hindrances to Liberation. And, in my own Quaker tradition, we are also urged to recognise the dangers of busyness. The following advice is taken from our *Quaker Faith and Practice*:

> Every stage of our lives offers fresh opportunities. Responding to divine guidance, try to discern the right time to undertake or relinquish responsibilities without undue pride or guilt. Attend to what love requires of you, which may not be great busyness.[14]

Of course, you may think that I am proposing a way of inaction, of distancing ourselves from the world and doing nothing. That is not so. Rather, I am proposing that we distinguish more clearly between what we might call Distracted Action and True Action. The former is common and the latter is rare. In the Parable of the Talents, Yeshua makes it clear that we have a duty to use our talents.[15] And in the opening chapters of the *Gita*, the Lord Krishna instructs the prince Arjuna that he has no option but to be active. Indeed, he teaches him that each one of us has a vocation – a way of life that is the true expression of our nature – and that this vocation is inescapable and cannot be set aside. However, it is also made clear that this *svadharma* can only be realised with the discipline, love and understanding that flow from a pure mind and a pure heart. It is in this way, and only in this way, that our *karma* can be transformed into True Action.[16]

I suppose this realisation of the importance of quietude should not come as a surprise to me since, as a birthright Quaker, my childhood was founded upon regular periods of silence, both in the local Meeting House and, indeed, at home, where my father's after-lunch naps and Sunday afternoon sleep were sacrosanct. Silence was the punctuation of our lives, the spaces in between, the commas and the full stops of the everyday. I gave it no thought. It was all I knew. But now, so much later and in the midst of cacophony and unrest, I realise I was given a Great Gift. And it is expressed in this extract from a passage written by the American Quaker mystic, Rufus Jones, in 1926. He was speaking of his youth:

> While I was too young to have any religion of my own, I had to come to a home where religion kept its fires as always burning. We had very few things, but we were rich in invisible wealth. I was not christened in the church, but I was sprinkled from morning to night with the dew of religion. We never ate a meal which did not begin with a hush of thanksgiving; we never began a day without a family gathering at which mother read a chapter of the Bible after which there would follow a weighty silence. These silences, during which all the children of our family were hushed with a kind of awe, were very important features of my spiritual development. There was work inside and outside the house waiting to be done, and yet we sat there hushed and quiet, doing nothing. I very quickly discovered that something real was taking place. We were feeling our way down to that place from which living words come, and very often they did come.[17]

I am writing this passage in February 2021. We are still in Covid Lockdown. It all began nearly a year ago, when it was commonly supposed that the restrictions that were imposed would last perhaps a couple of months. But they have persisted and then The Virus has mutated to a more quickly spreading form. The wearing of masks has now become widely accepted, social distancing is part of our lives, and we have all reduced the amount we travel. At Christmas many families were separated at the very time when they would expect to gather together, and on New Year's Eve there were no public firework displays, just a few families letting off rockets and Catherine-wheels in their gardens. It is a world we have not known before, and now it is everywhere.

Vaccines are being given to more and more people, but there seems little prospect of immunity for everyone in anything like the short term. Speaking to friends on Zoom, we talk about the ways in which this has changed our lives, perhaps forever. Are we hoping to return to the way things were before The Virus, taking up once again our old habits; or are we, inevitably, being moved towards another way of being? Quite early on, I cannot remember exactly when or where, I read an article by two young Chinese scientists that said that The Virus was not an enemy, it was a messenger, that it was Nature's way of telling us that we had to stop what we were doing; that in forcing us to change, it was showing us what this 'other way' would be like – had to be like – slow down, consume less, travel less, give greater respect both to all other people and to Nature herself. If that is true, then any attempt to return to how things were before may be foolish and unlikely to succeed.

But how does this relate to the matter of Silence and Love? It seems to me that all that has happened, all that we are being shown, requires the deepening of the practice of Silence, especially Gathered Silence.

During these recent months, my local Quaker Meeting has been unable to meet in person, and so some of us have taken to meeting via Zoom. From quite early on in lockdown we began meeting every Tuesday morning for half an hour of Gathered Silence followed by what we call After Words, a period in which we can share with each other thoughts and feelings that have either arisen in the previous week or have arisen during our time of Silence. To start with we all felt the same unease and uncertainty at this form of gathering, but quite soon, since those attending became a small but constant group, we became familiar with the practice and, indeed, began to experience a quality of Silence that was different from usual. There was something about meeting from our own homes and being able to see not only everyone else but also ourselves within the Zoom 'gallery view', that deepened the experience, bound us together.

Perhaps because a number of our group were living alone, in an isolation intensified by forced separation, to begin with there was quite often an outpouring of emotion as Friends (as we Quakers call each other) shared their suffering at being unable to be with others and with family, to be living without any physical touch. But as the weeks and then the months went by something else happened. The Silence became deeper. And it began to change us. It began to heal us. The solitude of lockdown took us to another place, a place in which we were surrendering to the stillness and silence, shedding parts of whom we had been.[18]

I can only explain this – insofar as it needs explaining – in my way, and I cannot tell whether this will make sense to anyone else. But for me, it has made me realise that in Silence – and without words – we may be discovering something important about our true selves; that stillness and silence are more of who we truly are than restlessness and noisiness; that we were silent before we spoke; that we were slow before we became pacey; and that if silence has always been there, hidden away in small places, now it is spreading, now it is being found everywhere. For, it seems to me that like Love, Silence, too, is of the essence, the true realm of all that is.

There are many views of what Silence is.[19] Some speak of it being in the underlying silence of Nature or that it is to be found in sculpture and painting or in music, silence being the intervals between the separate and gathered sounds. It is there in the cloister and in the lives and stories of hermits and those who pray, not least those who say the Hesychast's prayer, prayer without ceasing. Some present Silence as if it were an absence, a blank page, an entirely interior experience, a withdrawal. But that is not how I find it. For me, Silence is a presence, an ever-moving energy or force that permeates all that is both within and beyond. It courses through the Cosmos and it courses through each one of us. It is rather like water, which flows everywhere and finds the niches and cracks before pouring through, and which is sometimes hidden underground. It is in every cloud and raindrop, in every river and in the great oceans, and it runs through trees and plants and through the arteries and

And Then There Was Silence…

veins of our bodies and all that is. And it is as much in the muddy puddle as the clear stream. This is what Silence is like when we step into it.

I had a dream the other night, which was quite unlike the dreams that I normally have, full of anxiety, missing trains and being in the wrong place, or wearing the wrong clothes. In this unexpected dream, I experienced a profound acceptance of Love, a form of grace that flowed into me because I was open, utterly open. Perhaps that is what Love sometimes requires, a still and open place into which it can flow.

And so, as we try to come to terms with what The Virus is telling us, I have a sense, that we are now being asked to return to this place of Repose, this place of Silence that Mary Magdalene spoke of, both to learn what has already been said about it and to experience it anew in every moment of our lives. To strike a new balance between action and words and stillness and quietude.

And this brings me back to my life as a Quaker.

Quakers worship in silence, but the silence is not just the context for worship, it *is* the worship, which is to say that the worship is a kind of surrendering to Silence. It is a kind of waiting, not in the sense of anticipating but simply being there. At this point, I should say, of course, that I cannot speak for Quakers as a whole. No Friend can do that, for there is no Quaker doctrine, no creed, no priest to tell us what the Church requires. Rather, I speak for myself, for the experiences I had as a child and while growing up, and for the experience I now have with local Friends in this part of Suffolk.

Quakers are very careful with words. Within the setting of Gathered Silence, there may be ministry, when someone in the meeting will stand to speak, to 'bear witness'; but, in accordance with the only book of guidance that we have, *Quaker Faith and Practice* – which includes guidance, reflections and what are called 'Advices and Queries' – Friends are advised to think carefully before speaking and never to speak for too long. "Beware," says Advice 13, "of speaking predictably or too often, and of making additions towards the end of a meeting when it was well left before."[20] And when one Friend speaks, the others gathered there are asked to listen attentively. When the Friend has spoken, there should be a period of silence

before anyone else speaks, and even then, their ministry should not
be in the form of a rebuttal or even an acclamation of what had just
been said. Breaking the silence is significant, and no-one should do
it without feeling sure that what they have to say is being called for.

This careful practise is called 'right ordering' and it applies
not only to regular meetings for worship but also to all meetings,
including business meetings in which the minutes of the meeting
are agreed there and then as we go along, one item at a time. What
is written down is shared with Friends until all are content with it.
There is never a vote, the purpose of the minute being simply to
record 'the feeling of the meeting'. Silence pervades the meeting,
and no voice will be ignored. If a minute cannot be agreed, Friends
will either move into silence and try again, or leave the matter until
another time when they will have been able to reflect upon what
is best. You might think that this would mean that decisions are
delayed, but in my experience this is seldom the case, and, knowing
they will be heard, Friends most often find agreement. Throughout
such meetings, which are themselves regarded as meetings for
worship, Silence is ever-present, it is the realm in which decisions
are made. And this is because the Silence is active. It is not a context
for what might otherwise be no more than a muted hearing, it is the
very substance within which Friends speak and listen thoughtfully.

Amongst Friends, this sense of an orderly Silence is found in
the following extract from a meeting held in Wiltshire in 1678. The
meeting was one in which, in each quarter of the year, Friends would
have gathered to consider the life of their local meetings. This extract
sets down "Advice on the conduct of meetings for church affairs:"

Wherefore let whatever is offered, be mildly proposed, and so
left with some pause, that the Meeting may have opportunity to
weigh the matter, and have a right sense of it, that there may be
a unanimity and joint concurrence of the whole. And if anything
be controverted, that it be in coolness of Spirit calmly debated,
each offering their reasons and sense, their assent or dissent, and
so leave it without striving. And also that but one speak at once,
and the rest hear. And that private debates and discourses be
avoided, and all attend the present business of the Meeting. So

And Then There Was Silence ...

will things be carried on sweetly as becomes us, to our comfort: and love and unity be increased: and we better serve Truth and our Society.[21]

Here the matter of silence is touched with a necessary gentleness and an attentive listening. Things are "carried on sweetly." "True silence," said William Penn in 1699, "is to the spirit what sleep is to the body, nourishment and refreshment."[22] And later, in words that speak of Silence as a refuge, John Bellows, in 1895, said:

> I know of no other way, in these deeper depths, of trusting in the name of the Lord, and staying upon God, than in sinking into silence and nothingness before Him... So long as the enemy can keep us reasoning he can buffet us to and fro; but into the true solemn silence of the soul before God he cannot follows us.

There is something attractive, even comforting, in the apparent certainty of faith in these Quakers of another time, although I have to confess that I do not share their anthropomorphic reference to God as singular and male. My 'God' is without gender and without form, something more akin to an Ultimate Reality, an expression of a mysterious and deep Love. But I share their intent, which I think is captured in these more recent (1937) words, again of Rufus Jones:

> [The early Friends] made the discovery that silence is one of the best preparations for communion [with God] and for the reception of inspiration and guidance. Silence itself, of course has no magic. It may be just sheer emptiness, absence of words or noise or music. It may be an occasion for slumber, or it may be a dead form. But it may be an intensified pause, a vitalised hush, a creative quiet, an actual moment of mutual and reciprocal correspondence with God.[24]

The great spiritual traditions have always understood the need for attentive silence, for the regular practice of meditation and contemplation. For such a practice is regarded as the very foundation of true action. Indeed, as the late Greek orthodox writer, Philip Sherrard, has made clear, silent contemplation is the foundation upon which all else stands. Suggesting that true knowledge requires us to become one with the divine, Sherrard proposes that this must be through the practice of contemplation:

> ... For contemplation is essentially the action through which we are led to a knowledge of our true identity and being and hence the true identity and being of other things as well... It is not (then) that contemplation is opposed to action: Not only is it in itself a form – the highest form – of action, but also unless all other actions are informed by the knowledge that it embraces they will be performed in ignorance... To act well, we must first know. Thus, while contemplation and action are complementary, they are not on an equal footing: contemplation must precede action.[26]

And for those who have had the privilege of living, even for a short while, with those that most patently lead a holy life, it will be clear that the distinction between contemplation and action is a false one. Indeed, by contrast, it seems to me that it is our thoughtless and compulsive urge to 'do' that so often leads to harm.

Huxley's *Perennial Philosophy* had something to say about this attentive contemplation, the still and clear tranquillity of meditation. Indeed, in Chapter 3 is the following quotation from the great Chinese figure, Lao Tzu, the author of *The Tao Te Ching*:

> Those who know don't talk.
> Those who talk not know.[27]

So, there we have it – slowness, stillness, silence and attentiveness. How different all this seems from the unending noise, pace and destruction of today. In this, I note with some amusement that writing in 1945 Huxley says:

And Then There Was Silence...

The twentieth century is, among other things, the Age of Noise. Physical noise, mental noise and the noise of desire – we hold history's record for all of them. And no wonder; for all the resources of our almost miraculous technology have been thrown into the current assault against silence. That most popular and influential of all recent invention, the radio, is nothing but a conduit through which prefabricated din can flow into our homes.[28]

One wonders what he would have said today with television and the intrusive compulsion of mobile phones, not to mention the constant noise of aeroplanes and traffic near and distant.

But this morning I woke, as I often do, at about a quarter past five. Everything was still and silent. I opened the curtains of my bedroom and lay in bed, my head propped on my pillow so that I could look out into the garden and watch the light come. The silence was everywhere, and I let myself rest within it. And then I remembered these words spoken by Anne Baring in an interview we did together for the Spirit of Humanity Forum. [29] When I got up, I checked the recording:

> Love is the Pulse of the Cosmos and the pulse of our own deepest nature. We are all connected to each other and to the Earth and the Cosmos through our participation in a miraculous Web of Life. If we can become aware that Love is the deepest, most essential quality of our nature, we will strengthen our capacity to radiate love to the planet, and to each other, and to heal the immense suffering of the world. We urgently need a New Story that would provide a different context for addressing all our problems, a different vantage point from which to approach them – utterly different from the one that has prevailed for millennia. We need to relinquish old habits of power, rivalry, control and dominance and old beliefs that have divided us, and define a new spirituality grounded in Reverence for Life.
>
> The New Story, coming to us from the astounding discoveries of quantum physics, tells us that we are indissolubly connected to each other, to the life of the planet and the life

of the cosmos. Embracing this New Story asks us to develop what mystics call the Eye of the Heart, serving a new image of Spirit that is not remote from this world but immanent in every aspect of it – the invisible ground of the entire manifest universe and the ground of our own consciousness. We are not separate from Spirit, but co-creators with it. This gives us the immense responsibility of caring for the life around us with new insight, new compassion and new vision.

So, to find Love, we must attend to our Language and find the time to step into Silence. Is this the realm of The Divine?

I am learning from listening to the teachings of the Jungian Analyst, Brenda Crowther,[30] that when we come to The Divine, we have to distinguish between 'God' and 'The God Image'. The former is the unknowable and universal reality, the cosmic consciousness. The latter is the ways in which this unknowable source is manifested in different times and places, The Buddha, Yahweh, Jesus Christ, and so on. This latter form changes over time, or may change over time, and in our present time is being expressed in forms that I would call Love and the Divine Feminine, and perhaps this is leading us to a place where, once again, we shall discover an intertwining of the Divine Feminine and the Divine Masculine in the Great Divine.

And Then There Was Silence…

Endnotes

1. T. S. Eliot, East Coker, *Four Quartets*, Faber and Faber, Tenth impression, 1979, 24-25.

2. The Buddhist teaching on Mindfulness is set out in MN 10 and 118 and an excellent teaching is also given by Larry Rosenberg in his book *Breath by Breath*, Shambhala, 1998.

3. I regret that I can no longer find this reference.

4. Annemarie Schimmel, *As Through a Veil: Mystical Poetry in Islam*, Oneworld Publications, 2001, 97.

5. Op cit, *The Bhagavad Gita*, 84.

6. Jean-Yves Leloup, *The Gospel of Mary Magdalene*, Inner traditions, 2002, 37.

7. *The Essential Rumi*, Translated by Colman Barks, Penguin Books, London, 1995, 17.

8. Geoffrey Hubbard, 1974, quoted in *Quaker Faith and Practice*, Fourth Edition, The Yearly Meeting of the Religious Society of Friends (Quakers) in Britain, 1995-2008, 26.12.

9. *The Dhammapada*, Penguin Classics, 1973, 64. 15.205.

10. Op Cit, *The Bhagavad Gita*, 29. 5.27 and 28.

11. *Rumi, Mathnawi*, ed. R. A. Nicholson, Chapter 1 Lines 112-15. Quoted in Annemarie Schimmel, *As Through a Veil: Mystical Poetry in Islam*, Oneworld Publications, 2001, 101.

12.   Michael Leunig, *The Curly Pyjama Letters*, Viking, 2001.

13.   Ibid.

14.   Op cit, *Quaker Faith and Practice*, Advice 28.

15.   Matthew 25 14-30.

16.   See *The Bhagavad Gita*, Penguin Classics, 1962, translated by Juan Macasró, especially chapters 2-5; and Vinoba, *Talks on the Gita*, published by Sarva Seva Sangh Prakashan, 14th edition, November 2000, especially chapters 2-5.

17.   Rufus Jones, *Quaker Faith and Practice*, The Yearly Meeting of the Religious Society of Friends, London, Fourth Edition, 1995-2008, 21.01.

18.   Reviewing this text for publication in August 2022, I can report that we continue to meet every Tuesday.

19.   See, for example: Alain Corbin, *A History of Silence*, Polity, 2019, Robert Sardello, *Silence: The Mystery of Wholeness*, Goldstone Press, Heaven and Earth Publishing and North Atlantic Books, 2006 and Max Picard, *The World of Silence*, Eight Day Press, 2002, first published in 1948.

20.   Op Cit, *Quaker Faith and Practice*, Advice 13.

21.   Op Cit, *Quaker Faith and Practice*, 19.57.

22.   Ibid. 2.13.

23.   Ibid. 2.15.

24.   Ibid. 2.16.

And Then There Was Silence...

25.   Philip Sherrard, *Christianity, Lineaments of a Sacred Tradition*, T&T Clark, 1998.

26.   Ibid. 246-7.

27.   *Tao Te Ching*, translated by Stephen Mitchell, Kyle Cathie, 2000.

28.   Op cit, Huxley, 249-250.

29.   See davidcadmanatwork.com/thoughts.

30.   In her webinar series of Jung and his Red Book on the Ubiquity University website:ubiquityuniversity.org.

Introduction to Part Two

Having explored the matter of Language, the Meaning of Love and the necessary practise of Silence, I now want to takes us to the voices of women, both in their ancient form as goddesses and in their present form as being amongst those who challenge the dominance of patriarchy and offer us different visions of the future. When this is done, we shall be ready – I hope – to look at possible future pathways, or, at least, to look at some of those that have been of interest to me, and which I would like to share with you. These are pathways that lead to the possibility of what I would call A Way of Love, which I will explore in the Final part of this book, in Reflections.

CHAPTER FOUR

The Divine Feminine

As an elderly man looking back over my life, I now realise – although
I did not know it before – that I have spent my life seeking the
Divine Feminine, the Goddess and the Great Mother. It is as if I have
always known she was missing, and now understand how much she
is needed. She has always been there whenever I have unknowingly
turned towards her, often there in friends and colleagues and in my
closest companions. I thought it was personal, but now, I realise that
it was not, that I have been and am drawn to the deepest yearning
of the Cosmos, the widespread longing for something lost. And now,
as patriarchy begins to degenerate and fall apart – for that's what is
happening – we are seeing all around us once more the re-emergence of
the feminine seeking a rightful presence with the masculine. Coming
to be, coming to be, ceasing to be, ceasing to be.[1] I think that is why I
came eventually to live by the sea and by a tidal river, for the Goddess
has always been associated with water and with sea.

I knew this when I was writing *Love and the Divine Feminine*. And
now I have come to see that it has always been the Goddess who we
have turned to when we have needed to feel the touch of the Divine,
especially the Mother Goddess who is grounded and immanent. The
Father God, in many forms, has always been presented as more remote
and at a distance. I feel this deeply. In moments of intimacy, which can
be both nurturing or scary, we have needed the Goddess – as we do
now, for now we need the qualities that she brings, a strange mixture of
fierceness and compassion.

As I have already said, in *Love and the Divine Feminine* I asked
the question of how it is that we have come to be who we are. I
have asked this question many times before, and now I ask it again.
Within the context of the dilemmas of this twenty-first century –
faced with a climate emergency, in the midst of a global pandemic,
and with the presence of hatred and division in political life – how
is it that we have seemingly turned a blind eye to manifest harm and
injustice? As I suggested in the Introduction, it seems to me that this
has happened because of two losses: the loss of Love and the loss of the
Divine Feminine. And more and more, I now see that these two are
inextricably intertwined.

We have, so far, spoken of Love, but what can we say of the
Goddess.

As *Love and the Divine Feminine* records,[2] over the last 4,000 to 5,000 years, the realm of the Goddess has been rejected, abandoned and suppressed by an all-conquering and often demonising patriarchy, replacing a culture of integration and immanence with one of domination and separation, eventually with a single male God dwelling not amongst us but above us in the sky, our only way of reaching him being though accepting our innate sinfulness and seeking redemption through the institution of an all-male Church. This damaging Christian doctrine of original sin, when matched by the demonisation of the feminine in the story of Eve, and then in the life of the institutional Church in its exclusion of women, has brought us to where we are. Whilst the true Christian church, the church of the saints and the mystics, those who followed the Wisdom teachings and the teachings of Proverbs and the Song of Songs, may have remained in the realm of Love, those who took charge of the Church, those who sought power, those who governed, most certainly did not. They turned to inquisition and violence in the face of what they took as heresy, and came to justify war and slaughter in the name of God. Regrettably, since their voice has been the loudest and the most strident, it has brought us here, all but broken and in great danger.

If, then, we must find another place, another way of being, we must restore Love, and to do this we must restore the Divine Feminine. Without this, we will not be able to heal our wounds, we will not be able to bring ourselves back into alignment with the Cosmos, with that Nature of which we are a part. And for this, for Love to flow, we must bring back, and reintegrate, the Divine Feminine, we must enable her voice to he heard, and attend to what she says.

But what is this voice?

The story of the goddesses is wonderfully set out in one of the books most quoted in *Love and the Divine Feminine*, Anne Baring's and Jules Cashford's *The Myth of the Goddess*,[3] and in its Preface, the late Sir Laurens Van Der Post talks of those parts of our history which remain hidden. He says:

There is no dimension of history of which this is more true than the way the feminine half of the human spirit has been dealt with by masculine-dominated societies, and inadequately acknowledged and evolved in our cultures and civilizations."[4]

I am very much taken with this, and I observe it in all that has happened and still happens around me, most especially in the way that women have been, or rather have not been, valued and heard. But this is not the limit of my concern, for, as an elderly man, I feel the loss in my own being, too. The loss of the Divine Feminine is important to me as a man, for the feminine is beyond sexual identity. With her loss, some part of who I am as a man is denied. I acknowledge that the evident prejudice and mistreatment suffered by women is much more important than what has happened to me, but with the loss of the Divine Feminine we share this loss – men and women alike – we share in this loss, and it has made all of us who we are.

There is a pattern that we see all about us in Nature: the cycle of birth, life, death and renewal. It seems to be a necessary part of all that is, not least ourselves. And then there is the cycle of the seasons and the cycles of Moon[5] with her waxing and waning and her period of darkness. Here in coastal Suffolk, living as I do beside the North Sea, I see this in the turning of the waves on the shingle as the waters move up the beach; I see it in the tides, flooding and ebbing in the river Alde, and that point at the turn of the tide when, for a brief moment, everything seems to stand still. Darkness gives way to light, winter gives way to spring, and then come summer and autumn before the darkness returns. It was these patterns and these cycles, that must have caused our ancestors to feel such a sense of awe, wonder – and, perhaps, fear – that they worshipped whatever it was or whoever it was that they believed made all this happen. They called her Goddess, and one of the earliest images that we have found, the Goddess of Laussel, in the Dordogne area of France, shows a female form with wide belly and hips, and full breasts, holding what seems to be a crescent moon. This Is the Palaeolithic Mother goddess of some 20,000 BCE. According to Anne Baring and Jules Cashford:

The Divine Feminine

Long ago, some 20,000 years ago and more, the images of a
goddess appeared across a vast expanse of land stretching from
the Pyrenees to Lake Baikal in Siberia. Statues in stone, bone
and ivory, tiny figures with long bodies and falling breasts,
rounded motherly figures pregnant with birth, figures with
signs scratched upon them – lines, triangles, zigzags, circles,
nets, leaves, spirals, holes – graceful figures rising out of rock
and painted with red ochre – all these have survived through
the unrecorded generations of human beings who compose the
history of the race.[6]

But in time, and much later, we come to goddesses who have
qualities that go well beyond their fertility, goddesses such as the
Egyptian goddess, Ma'at, who was the goddess of balance and order;
or Metis, the Greek goddess, who was worshipped for her wisdom,
her healing power and her cunning; or the clear-sighted Hecate
who ruled over earth, sea and sky and helped give direction. And,
again in time, many of the goddesses had a consort, as if to integrate
the feminine with the masculine, the hunter with the mother – in
Sumeria Ki and An, and then Dumuzid and Inanna; and, later, Isis
and Osiris in Egypt.

But then, by the time we come to the last millennium BCE,
when Zeus and the Olympians rule, the older goddesses are already
on the wane. They have been diminished and replaced by, or are now
ruled by, gods. Thus, Metis is swallowed by Zeus, who then gives
birth to Athena as a father's daughter, assertive, a goddess not only
of wisdom but of warfare. Hestia the goddess of the hearth and fire
is eventually replaced with the god Dionysus. The essential nature
of the goddess as being wise and bringing order and balance is lost. I
regret this. I am not really drawn to the strident Athena, nor to the
young Aphrodite, although Botticelli's 'Primavera' and his 'Birth of
Venus' are both of exceptional beauty. And I wonder if these figures
are not misrepresentations of the older and the more subtle and
mysterious qualities of the goddess. I like the wisdom and cunning
of Metis, the balance of Maat and the clear sightedness of Hecate,
but it is Hestia, the older sister of Zeus, that I hold in my heart. It is
she who gives me comfort. Can I be forgiven for that? It's just that

I am finding that comfort becomes more appealing as I get older.

By the time we come to the stories set out in the Bible, goddesses are publicly banished and profane. In a world that would one day shape mine, the Judeo-Christian world into which I would be born, there was now to be One God, Yahweh, and he was male and without a consort. And yet, it was not quite as straightforward as that. For the goddesses persisted, sometimes hidden and then emerging. It was not as if my forbears, and perhaps yours, went to sleep one night worshipping goddesses and gods and woke up the next morning worshipping only Yahweh. The change, though dramatic, at first came about slowly, especially amongst the common people who were reluctant to give up the divine world they had inherited from their parents and grandparents.

Significant was the goddess Asherah,[7] who was the consort of Anu or, in another form, of El, the god who preceded Yahweh, the God who is spoken of in the story of the Garden of Eden. Asherah was the queen consort and her son was Baal. She was a mother goddess, a goddess of the sea. And the poles by which she was worshipped are referred to in the Old Testament.[8] It seems clear that, despite the command to love only One God, the jealous God, Yahweh, she continued to be worshipped, much to the anger of the Hebrew priests and prophets who condemned her and wished to destroy her. Nevertheless, it is possible that for some people she remained as the wife of Yahweh, being more accessible, and worshipped at harvest times.[9] It is even possible that Solomon made burnt sacrifices to her.[10] And once he had gone, his son Rehoboam again supported the worship of Asherah, his favourite wife, Maacah, being devoted to the goddess.[11] Indeed, Asherah's pole stood at the alter of Yahweh in the Temple in Jerusalem, until It was removed and burnt by Asa, a later king of Judah.

And even then, although the texts are contradictory, it is possible that the people continued to worship Asherah's poles.[12] Certainly, Jezebel, the much-reviled wife of King Ahab, is supposed to have returned to the worship of both Asherah and her son Baal. And, it would seem that later, after being once more abandoned, she returned again, because the common people would not let her go. Indeed, it would seem that they persisted until the most 'reforming' priests of all, the Deuteronomists, finally prevented her being worshipped. But even then, there remained lingering shadows of the goddess in the feminine qualities of Wisdom represented in Christian gnosticism by Sophia,[13] and in the Shekinah of the Jewish Kabbalah.[14]

And then of course, in the New Testament, the feminine presence of the divine appears in Mary, the Mother of Yeshua.[15] She takes little part in the story between the annunciation, the nativity and the crucifixion, and yet, within five hundred years of her own death, images of her as a goddess began to appear. Indeed, in some parts of the Great Church, midst dispute, she was referred to her as 'God-bearer'.[16] In the fifteenth century, in what might well have been regarded as a heretical image, the carved and painted French Vierge Ouvrante triptych, now in the Paris Musée du Louvre, Mary was declared to be the Great Mother Goddess. When the doors of the triptych are opened:

> Mary is the declared Great Mother Goddess in whose body lives God, the Father, as her son, holding the cross of destiny for Christ, his son.[17]

When the triptych is closed, Mary returns to her more familiar posture of the human mother:

> …with the divine child who is to redeem the sin of the world-apple of Eve, which Mary, as the second Eve, holds in her hand.[18]

Doctrinally, this would be heresy, but such images of Mary are brought to life in ancient imagery:

> Here she is drawn as the Great Mother of Life and Death, Queen of Heaven, Earth and Underworld, Goddess of the Animals and Plants, and Goddess of the Wisdom of the Soul.[19]

She stands in the tradition of the great goddesses before her, virgin and mother, giving birth to a divine child who dies and is reborn.[20] And, in her emergence within the Christian church, it is as if the people would not be denied their goddess. Sometime between AD 400 and 500, the Temple of Isis in Soissons in France, was dedicated to 'the Blessed Virgin Mary'.[21] But it was in the twelfth century that the cult of Mary reached its height. With many churches and cathedrals being built in her honour, it would seem that there was a widespread sense that something was missing from the representation of the Divine; and this pressure continued into the twentieth century when in various papal declarations the all-but divine nature of Mary was accepted. She was the people's goddess. As Anne Baring and Jules Cashford say:

> How else to make sense of the constant debate over Mary lasting hundreds and hundreds of years, gathering to a crescendo in the last 150 years, which is essentially a debate on how human, or divine, she was and is? Why would it matter whether Mary was a goddess or not unless there was an overwhelming need to include an image of the feminine in the conception of the divine?[22]

And then, there is another aspect of this which brings together the matter of Love and the Divine Feminine. The teachings of Yeshua as they are described in both the Bible and in later gnostic texts such as *The Gospel of Thomas* and *The Gospel of Mary Magdalene* are teachings of Love that embrace and include both women and men – although, of course, they would in time be contorted into the grim doctrine of sin and redemption brought about by a cruel crucifixion and a miraculous resurrection: He died to save us all. Yeshua would have wept at this distortion, unless, of course, it is to be read metaphorically as the victory of Love.

One victim of this male domination was the very person who had been his beloved disciple, Mary Magdalene, for hundreds of years wickedly portrayed by the Great Church as a repentant prostitute. And in her own lifetime, Mary had to flee from Palestine, carrying with her the teachings of Love. But the damage had been done, and it is only now, two thousand years later, that she is being rediscovered in a wide spectrum of texts, some fantastical and some scholarly. But, as I said in *Love and the Divine Feminine*,[23] the interesting question is not which of these is or is not true, but why

The Divine Feminine

they are arising? There is no reason why I should have the answer to that question, but can it be that in our troubled times, faced with the degradation and destruction of Nature, we are, once more, seeking a divine figure that dwells not far from us in the sky, but right here in and around us, a Goddess of the Earth, a Mother Goddess of birth, love and compassion, bringing the possibility of healing and divine collaboration? I think that this is so and that we shall now discover in the teachings of Love the full wisdom of the Divine Feminine.

Endnotes

1.   These are the words spoken by the Buddha when he awoke from his deep meditation beneath the Bodhi tree.

2.   Op cit, David Cadman, 2020, 18-43.

3.   Anne Baring and Jules Cashford, *The Myth of the Goddess: Evolution of an Image*, Viking Arcana, 1991.

4.   Ibid. ix.

5.   I have deliberately dropped the use of the article 'the' here and have used a capital 'M' to denote the intimate and personal relation we have with Moon.

6.   Ibid. 3.

7.   Op cit, Lauri Martin Gardner, 10 et seq.

8.   Judges 6:25.

9.   Lauri Martin-Gardner, *The Hidden Goddess*, Moon Books, 2020, 10 et seq.

10.   Ibid. 13.

11.   Ibid. 15.

12.   Ibid. 15-16. See 1 Kings and 2 Chronicles.

13.   Anne Baring and Jules Cashford, *The Myth of the Goddess: Evolution of an Image*, Viking Arcana, 1991, 470-8.

14.   Ibid. 638-43.

15.   Ibid. 547-608.

16.   Ibid. 550.

17.   Ibid. 547.

18.   Ibid.

19.   Ibid.

20.   Ibid. 548.

21.   Ibid. 551.

22.   Ibid. 554.

23.   Op cit, David Cadman, 2020, 58.

CHAPTER FIVE

The Wrong Turning

Of all the representations of the integration of the feminine and masculine energies or qualities, the one that has most intrigued me has been the stories of the threefold nature of woman and man – Maiden, Queen and Crone, and Young Knight, King and Old Man. In these stories it is always the Old Man and the Crone, who are the most interesting and powerful. They both bring wisdom, and in the case of the Crone, it is she who transforms; it is she who begins and ends all adventures.

She appears in this form in two of my own stories (written under the name of William Blyghton). In *The Great Queen and the Gatekeeper's Son*,[1] she appears at the beginning of the story as the woman who forces into action the bereft courtiers who have lost first their Queen and then their King. And in *The King Who Lost His Memory*,[2] it is she who terrifies the King into action and is then there at the end to bring him home. In Celtic mythology she is Ceridwen, the mother of the poet, Taliesin; she is the goddess of change, transformation, wisdom and rebirth. Her threefold nature is seen in the waxing and waning of the moon, followed by her time in the period of darkness before the next new moon rises, darkness and then renewal. And it is the Crone whom men, especially powerful men, have most feared, treating wise women as if they were witches to be burnt and drowned. And not much of her is said in our time. We admire both the Maiden and the Queen, fecundity and motherhood, but we have almost nothing to say about the Crone. But, for me, it is the Crone who is most important, the most intriguing

So, here she is in another of my stories (again written in the name of William Blyghton), 'The Wrong Turning',[3] which speaks of the foolishness of Kings and their Advisors and of the wisdom of the Old Woman. It is a fable for our time, and for this book:

The King was sitting in his chamber and standing in front of him was a forlorn looking man, the King's Senior Advisor on Calamities and Things to Worry About. He was carrying a thick book, which he had opened at a particular page, and he had begun to address the King.

"I am sorry to have to say this, Your Majesty," he said, "but the findings of our latest report on 'What is Happening', that is the report prepared by your Majesty's Men in White Coats Who Know Everything, the findings of this report do not offer much comfort. It appears, Sir, that we took a wrong turning."

"A wrong turning," said the King, "whatever do you mean, a wrong turning?"

"Well, Sir," said the forlorn looking man, closing the book and placing it upon a table beside him, "your Men in White Coats are not sure when it was or how it came about, but they now see that some while ago, well, some while ago we took the wrong turning."

"There you go again," said the King, his voice rising with impatience. "There you go, you have said it again. That 'turning' thing, you have said it again. What do you mean, wrong turning?"

The Senior Advisor was now beginning to perspire and took from his pocket a large blue and white spotted handkerchief, with which he wiped his brow. He had begun to feel unwell.

"Your Majesty," he said in a voice that was beginning to creak, "would Your Majesty permit me to sit down for a moment."

"Sit down?" said the King, "Yes of course you can sit down. Why on earth would I worry if you were standing up or sitting down? Sit down. Sit down."

So the forlorn man, the Senior Advisor on Calamities and Things to Worry About, sat down and tried to recover himself.

"Might I trouble Your Majesty," he said, "for a glass of water?"

"Glass of water?" said the King, "Yes of course you can have a glass of water." And he rang a bell, which summoned a servant in blue stockings and a yellow tunic, who bowed low and asked the King what he would like.

"Bring this man a glass of water," said the King. "And while you are about it, bring me one, too. In fact, bring a jug of water and two glasses."

The servant bowed again and left the room, returning shortly with a tray upon which was a crystal jug of water and two glasses. He poured out a glass for the King and then, as was of course right, he poured a slightly smaller one for the Senior Advisor on Calamities and Things to Worry About.

For a minute or two neither the Senior Advisor nor the King said anything. The Advisor picked up his book and began to look at one or two of the pages, and the King, with a growing sense that things were not at all as they should be, stared at his shoes, noticing a scuffed patch on one of them.

"So," said the King looking once more at his Senior Advisor, "so what is this 'wrong turning' thing about?"

"Well Sir," said the Advisor now regaining his sense of importance and authority, "we thought it was all for the best. We thought that the more we could make and do, the better it would be for everyone. We thought that all the astonishing things we invented would make life better, richer, more completely wonderful. But I am sorry to say, Sir, very sorry to say, that this latest report by the Men in White Coats is saying that there were things that we didn't take into account. It seems to suggest that we didn't even think about them; that we were not even aware that we might have had to think about them. It was as if they were invisible to us. Not there at all."

The King was beginning to feel rather confused with all the things that apparently had not been taken into account or had not even been thought of, things which might have been invisible; and he was also beginning to fear that he was about to be told something very disagreeable, very disagreeable indeed. He took a drink from his glass and looked directly at his Advisor.

"You see," said the Advisor, "we had no idea how warm it might get and how stormy and wet, too."

"So is all this 'wrong turning' stuff and the things that you haven't thought of just about a little warmth and bit of rain?" said the King, now rather irritated that all his uneasiness might just have been caused by the possibility of a mere thunderstorm or two. "Heavens man, I know we had some flooding in the Autumn and that the Spring this year seems somewhat askew, but surely you are not suggesting that this amounts to one of your Calamities and Things to Worry About?"

"Well Sir," said the Advisor, "there was a time when we all thought that his was just as you have described it. Just some oddity in the weather. But...," and here he, too, took a drink from his glass, "but it seems, Sir, we were wrong."

"Wrong!" exclaimed the King, "Do you think I appoint people like

The Wrong Turning

you and the Men in White Coats that Know Everything to be wrong?"

"Well, you see, Sir," said the Advisor, now wishing he had not agreed to take on the task of reporting to the King, "there was a time when we, that is when the Men in White Coats, thought that the changes in our weather could just be kept within the limit of what they used to call Plus Two, but now," and he stopped, once more to drink from his glass, his hand shaking and spilling a little of the water on the floor, "but now, well now we know it will be, shall we say, somewhat worse than this. In fact, Sir, it could be, well it could be much worse. Some people, some of the men in White Coats that Know Everything, are now talking about what they call Plus Three."

The King was now listening with complete attention. His face was pale and his throat was dry. He could not move or speak. It was as if he had taken a thudding blow to his chest. He was not as ill informed as he sometimes pretended to be. And he had heard of this Plus Three, and he knew it was not at all good.

Not much more was said that day. The Senior Advisor departed leaving the King sitting in silence, his face set in a grim stare and his eyes fixed upon the thick book that the Advisor had left behind. He knew what he had to do. And he was not looking forward to it.

Early the next day before anyone else had woken, wrapped in the disguise of a long cloak with a hood, the King went out of his castle by a side door and set off for the forest beyond the castle grounds, following a path he had taken before. He was going to see the Old Woman who lived in a small and rather dark cottage in the middle of the forest. He was not looking forward to seeing her, but he knew he must.

He knew the path well and walked with his head down, not looking to the right or the left, deep in thought and with a growing sense of foreboding. He entered the forest and the path narrowed, twisting and turning its way to the middle. There he stopped. In front of him was the cottage of the Old Woman. A thin and turning spiral of smoke rising from the chimney suggested she was at home.

Reluctantly, the King walked up to the cottage door, threw back the hood of his cloak, and knocked. No reply. He knocked again, and then saw the Old Woman, dressed in what appeared to be a tattered eiderdown, coming towards him from the back of the cottage carrying a large bucket of water.

"Well, are you going to help me carry this bucket or not?" she said in a voice that was both ancient and sharp. "Could you for once in your stupid life not just stand about looking regal, but do something useful – like helping me carry this bucket? I am only carrying it because I knew you would come and see me and would need some tea; although I may not be able to find my kettle and I doubt I can tell you anything that will help you."

With that the Old Woman dropped the bucket to the ground, the water splashing onto what might have been shoes, but looked more like the husks of some kind of spiky animal.

The King hurried forward, taking up the bucket. It was surprisingly heavy, as if the water in it had come from somewhere deep in the ground. Carrying the bucket with both hands, he followed the Old Woman into her cottage, bending to pass through the low doorway. The room was as he remembered it, dark and with an earthen floor and an open fire, and with furniture covered with jars, tins, piles of old leaves and fruits, and with not just one but several cats draped asleep on shelves and sofas. One twitched an ear and opened one eye as the King came in.

"Put the bucket in the kitchen," commanded the Old Woman, "whilst I see if I can find a kettle." And with that she disappeared into a large cupboard from which came the sound of pots and pans being thrown this way and that, some of them falling to the ground with a great clatter. Eventually, the Old Woman reappeared clutching a large kettle covered with cobwebs. It had obviously not been used for a long time.

"I haven't used this kettle since you were last here with another one of your pitiful questions," said the Old Woman taking off the lid and waiting for the King to pour in some water. This done, the kettle was hung over the open fire to boil, whilst the Old Woman went off in search of a tin of tea, which she found tucked away under a pile of rags beside the sink.

"Now," said the Old Woman, "why don't we just sit down so that you can tell me all about the weather. I assume that is what you have come for." And with that she pushed one of the cats off the sofa and offered the seat to the King, whilst she sat upon a rocking chair beside the fire, setting it to rock slowly to and fro.

"Well," said the King, dreading what the Old Woman might say to him, "the Men in White Coats…"

But before he could continue, the Old Woman interrupted him.

"Good grief," she said, increasing the rocking of her chair, "don't tell me that these dullards have at last woken up to what anyone with half a brain could have seen ages ago! Don't tell me they have actually come to see what was staring them in the face."

"Well," continued the King, "it would seem that they have."

"Seem?" said the Old Woman, now rocking at a great pace, "What do you mean 'seem'?. They either have or they haven't. Which is it?"

"Well," said the King, somewhat flustered and alarmed at the rocking of the Old Woman's chair, "they have now seen that some while ago and for reasons that no-one quite knows, well that some while ago, we took a wrong turning."

"Wrong turning?" exclaimed the Old Woman with a crackling laugh, "Is that what they call it. Wrong turning, wrong turning!"

And she leapt out of the rocking chair and disappeared into the kitchen, from which there was again a great deal of clattering of china until she returned with a tray upon which was a large cream and crazed teapot and two mugs. She took the kettle from the fire and poured the hot water into the teapot. Then, having let it settle for a minute or two, she poured the tea into the two mugs, taking the larger one for herself, and giving the smaller one to the King. She was still chuckling to herself and repeating again and again the words, "wrong turning, wrong turning."

Once the mugs were filled with tea, or what might have been some brew of dubious and unknown provenance, the Old Woman climbed back into her rocking chair. But this time she stopped its rocking and leaning forward looked straight into the eyes of the King.

"Now listen to me," she said, "I shall say this once and only once, since I am tired of giving you advice that you ignore."

The King, too, sat forward and listened.

"You and your people have so disrupted this world with your selfishness, your hatred and your greed that what you call 'the weather' will never again be settled. Not in your lifetime, not in your children's lifetime, not in your grandchildren's lifetime and not in the lifetime of your grandchildren's grandchildren. Do you understand this?"

The King nodded his head but said nothing.

"There will be fires and dreadful storms of wind and rain, and the seas will rise to a great height. Many of you will not survive. Do you understand this?'

Again, the King nodded his head and said nothing.

"Now," said the Old Woman, "there is only one thing you can do. Are you listening?"

"Yes," said the King.

But what he heard took him by surprise.

"The only thing for you to do," said the Old Woman, "is to care for each other and to care for the Earth as if she was your Mother. Tenderness, kindliness and care. These are the qualities that you will need both to limit as much as you can the catastrophe that will come, and then to look after each other when the fire and the storms have swept many of you away."

She paused for a moment and set her eyes so deeply upon the King that he felt himself sinking into a deep and dark place, a place that at one and the same time both took away his breath and made him feel as if he had come home.

"I know," said the Old Woman, "that your Men in White Coats, your Bankers and your Advisors, will tell you this is nonsense and that all will be well with a slight change to business as usual, but then it was their advice that brought us to where we are; and you must remember that they can no longer hear the voice of the Earth. It's up to you."

And with that, the Old Woman got up from her chair, picked up the tray with the teapot and mugs, and disappeared into her kitchen, leaving the King staring into her fire.

 The Wrong Turning

The ending of this story is for you to decide upon. Do you think that the King took the advice of the Old Woman, or do you think that he just kept silent and let the Men in White Coats, the Bankers and the Advisors do as they wished? Do you think the fire and the storms and rain came? Do you think the seas rose to a great height? Or do you think these were just the ramblings of an Old Woman who couldn't find her kettle? Do you think the people of the King's realm learnt the lessons of love and a care for each other and the Earth, or do you think they, too, thought this was mere nonsense and just went on as usual?

Endnotes

1. William Blyghton, *Finding Elsewhere*, Panacea Books, 2018, 59 et seq. I have made some small revisions to the text.

2. Ibid. 37 et seq.

3. Ibid. 7 et seq.

CHAPTER SIX

Feminism and More

I hope you enjoyed the story of the King and the Old Woman in Chapter 5, and I wonder what you thought the ending was. But even talking in this way of the Divine Feminine and the Divine Masculine, and of the mythic threefold Woman and Man, can still leave us with feelings of separation and possibly opposition; and it leaves us without an answer to the final question set out in the Introduction:

> Is it useful to work with notions of 'the feminine' and 'the masculine' or do these notions create harmful divisions and cloud our understanding? And what would we be able to say about a discourse that was un-gendered, but which spoke of qualities to be found in all of us?

> How then might we begin to work toward an ungendered discourse, and what might it say?

To do this work, we must question and challenge those modes of thought that insist on separation and division. One such challenge, primarily concerned with matters of gender, comes from feminism. As an old man born into patriarchy and therefore undoubtedly shaped by it, I hesitate to speak of this voice, but I know that it is of the utmost importance. To deny it, would be to deny part of who we all are, and part of who I have become.

I asked my question about an ungendered discourse because I knew that gender prejudice was something that has been, and still is, a matter of great concern for women, and I wanted to hear their voice. However, until I began to look more closely, I did not know that, within feminism, there has been, and still is, a deep and long debate about the nature of this prejudice and how to challenge it, with many variations of view. Much of the debate has centred around the matter of 'essentialism', which is said to describe the troublesome view that we must take for granted that there are inherent, and somewhat fixed, qualities or characteristics of being a woman. As one writer has put it, essentialism is the view that:

> ...there are properties essential to women, in that any woman must necessarily have those properties to be a woman at all.[1]

In the 1970s and 1980s, many leading feminists rejected this view, and claimed that women could not be defined as a single category. One particular contribution to this debate came from Judith Butler, in her book *Gender Trouble*,[2] which was published in 1990. Observing the arguments amongst feminists about what it meant to be a woman, she questioned all fixed identities such as masculine/feminine or straight/gay, showing that 'sex', 'sexuality' and 'gender' are not the same thing, and that notions of 'gender' are very much socially constructed. If, for example, I were to follow her analysis, I would say that I am biologically male, have a preference for heterosexual relationships, but am fluid in terms of my gender, having a mixture of qualities that might otherwise be seen as masculine or feminine.

Later, in the 1990s, many feminists came to challenge ideas of anti-essentialism, since this was thought to limit the political possibility of women speaking as a distinct, disadvantaged and oppressed social group.[3] Then, in 2004, this point of view was itself challenged by Alison Stone, in a paper in which she explored the arguments for and against essentialism. Finding all of the earlier propositions to be problematic, she proposed her own idea of what she called 'genealogy', which suggested that whilst women were "a group with a distinctive, and distinctively oppressive, history,"[4] they lacked any common properties that constituted them all as women.[5] In this way, her notion of genealogy reconceived women as a determinate group "without reverting to the descriptive essentialist claim that all women share a common social position or mode of experience."[6]

Reconceiving women, and feminism, in this way, she said:

> ...provides a way for women to identify women as a definite

social group without falsely attributing to them any common characteristics that constitute them as women.[7]

And she went on to say:

> Thus, although women do not share any common characteristics, they are defined as a group by their participation in this history… [And] despite their lack of common characteristics, women can still exist as a determinate group, susceptible to collective mobilisation.[8]

This notion of women being defined by a shared history of oppression, may go some way to help us understand another element of contemporary feminism, which is the way in which women have increasingly seen themselves as part of a shared suffering. This is expressed in the notion of 'intersectionality' where women see themselves as part of a wider, and diverse, marginalised community, which also includes those who are racially and sexually marginalised. The term 'intersectional feminism' was first used in 1989 by an American woman, and civil rights activist, Kimberlié Crenshaw, and in a recent interview in *Time* magazine she said that it was:

> … a lens, a prism, for seeing the way in which various forms of inequality often operate together and exacerbate each other. We tend to talk about race inequality as separate from inequality based on gender, class, sexuality or immigrant status. What's often missing is how some people are subject to all of these, and the experience is not just the sum of its parts.[9]

So, now we have not only a feminism defined by the history of women's oppression, but a feminism that sees itself coming together with all other forms of marginalisation, a community of people of many kinds who are oppressed simply for being who they are.

This is a complex but understandable story of the ways in which one group of people, in this case women, have tried to express their opposition to an old, damaging and failing hegemony of persistent prejudice and ignorance; and how, through their own exploration of

Feminism and More

their differences, they have come to see themselves as part of a wider community of those who have also been, and are, oppressed. This tells us much about the broad and dominant reach of patriarchy, and how, even in its failing, it persists because it is so deeply embedded in our consciousness. This domination has prevented any voice other that its own from being heard, and, as we have already seen, its regimes of dominance are still found in politics, religion, education, commerce and healthcare. Indeed, the dominance remains so prevalent that we may often hardly notice it, but just assume that this is how things are.

Feminists are amongst those (including me) who find such a proposition utterly unacceptable. Now they are aligned with all who suffer, and this reinforces the feminist proposition that whilst there are many forms of oppression, they all have a root cause founded in the base qualities of patriarchy: dominance, selfishness, violence, divisiveness and control. In looking forwards we must assume that feminism will seek the removal of all these oppressions. Indeed, the National Organisation for Women has suggested that this would include:

> understanding that patriarchy is harmful to everyone; that all gender identities and sexualities should be respected and acknowledged; that all genders and races should be treated equally; and that all people should be treated with respect.[10]

Whilst patriarchy has been, and still is, a dominant language, we must, therefore, expect that as a growing number of women begin to be heard what is said will change. If they challenge the established patriarchy with a new voice, and if this voice is their own and not one distorted by patriarchy, then dialogue will change. If, at the same time, this means that all of those who have been marginalised will be able to speak, then this, too, will change what is said and heard, and a new discourse will arise. Another aspect of ourselves, men and women alike, will be voiced and this will, perhaps, begin to shape the future. This new language has not yet taken hold, but if, as seems at least possible, there is an aspect of our humanity that has been suppressed and is now to be expressed and listened to and honoured, nothing can be the same. None of us can be, will be, the same as we have been, and are.

In terms of the question that I asked at the beginning of this chapter about an 'ungendered discourse', one of the problems of feminism is sometimes said to be that in identifying itself as being a women's movement it points to the very division it contests, even if this division is somewhat removed in the more recent feminist focus on a single oppressed community, which includes men and women. In any event, the debate, and the struggle that goes with it, does show how difficult it is to tackle prejudice *with words already framed and defined by the oppressor*. This is where Judith Butler's work is of great help, since it raises the necessity to speak of what is normal and what is queer, or rather of what is said to be normal and queer.[11] This is important because, by implication, it also speaks of what is possible and what is not. As she puts in the 1999 Preface to *Gender Trouble*:

>...no political revolution is possible without a radical shift in one's notion of the possible and the real.[12]

Whilst I regard the work of feminists as being of the utmost importance, it seems to me unlikely that within their discussions and proposals there would be a place for my exploration of the Divine Feminine, since this might well be regarded as being caught in arcane perceptions, and as failing to address the contemporary and systemic nature of patriarchy. Indeed, this must be so, since even to speak of 'the feminine', even the Divine Feminine, would perhaps be regarded as slipping back into the rejected 'essentialism'. However, there are many other expressions of 'the feminine', by women, who may or may not classify themselves as feminist, but who are most certainly challenging the way things are. I have chosen to have a look at four: an American woman known as Starhawk;

Feminism and More

a woman writer, visionary and gardener living in Tasmania, Annie March; the renowned American author, the late Ursula K. Le Guin; and a woman living in the Devon, England, Lorna Howarth. Each of these women in their different ways offers us a view of another possible way of being, the first three set in the distant future.

Starhawk's website describes her as a practitioner of permaculture and Earth-based spirituality,[13] and her book, *The Fifth Sacred Thing*,[14] first published in 1993, describes a world divided in two. In the Northlands, there is a non-violent society who care for the Earth. Sexuality is fluid and abundant, but without prejudice and without traditional constraints. Couples, men and women alike, become close and sometimes exclusive, but only by consent and without domination. The lives of the people are centred around a right relationship with Four Sacred Things: air, fire, water and earth. It is said that none of these can be owned since they are given by Nature, and so they are shared. In the Southlands there is a tyrannical and violent society governed by the Stewards. Prophetically, since it was written over thirty years ago, the story tells of a virus that is deliberately spread by the Stewards,[15] who also manufacture, limit and control the antidote, breeding men to be soldiers and women to be whores. The time comes when the Northlands are threatened by the armies of the Southlands, but the Northlands' people defend themselves without the use of weapons, again and again speaking the following words to their enemies: "There is a place for you at our table."

In the Northlands, women and men together govern and heal, and it is the older women who have influence. The 'old crone' Maya speaks:

This moon brings a time of hope and danger: fire season. We watch the dry hills anxiously, knowing that the rains are weeks or months away. Those us who are old have seen the fire destroy our drought-baked cities and smoke eclipse the sun. We've seen rich croplands shrivel into glass-hard deserts, and the earth itself collapse on its emptied water table. We have seen diseases claim our children and our lovers and our neighbours. We know it can happen again.[16]

Now, in 2022, we know it has. All these things, fire and drought and pandemic are happening in our time.

In the story, Maya continues:

We hope for harvest, we pray for rain, but nothing is certain. We say the harvest will only be abundant if the crops are shared, that the rains will not come unless water is conserved and shared and respected.[17]

In the Northlands, each house has its water cistern and the sharing of water is governed by a Water Council.

We believe we can continue to live and thrive only if we care for one another. This is the age of the Reaper, when we inherit five thousand years of postponed results, the fruits of our callousness toward the earth and toward other human beings. But at last we have come to understand we are part of the earth, part of the air, the fire, and the water, as we are part of one another.[18]

And surely, that is what we are doing, living with "the fruits of our callousness toward the earth and toward one another."

The sequel to *The Fifth Sacred Thing* is *City of Refuge*, which was published twenty-two years later, in 2015.[19] Here the conflict remains, but now the author assumes that the people of the Southlands will have to go onto the offensive and resort to violence to defeat the Stewards. There is a popular rising of protest, but both the solution and the sexual relations are less tender. Nevertheless, in this woman's voice, the answer to the predicament of oppression in which people find themselves is broadly one of living with Nature, communal sharing, gender fluidity. Generosity and courage.

The matter of non-violence is also explored in Annie March's *Butterfly's Children*,[20] where she imagines a future world in which endemic male violence is no longer accepted as just being inevitable. It is diagnosed as 'Redound Syndrome', to be treated as an illness, an addiction, to be controlled by medication and social governance. In her notes, at the beginning of the book, the author explains Redound Syndrome (RS) as follows

The origins of RS, named for the way violence (enacted, or in extreme cases, intended), fatally rebounds on the perpetrator and causes death by endocrine meltdown, continue to baffle virologists. The virus is latent in all humans, yet unrelated to any known… pathogens. There is passionate speculation and furious scoffing over the possibility of an extra-terrestrial source.

RS continues to flare up sporadically across all cultures and populations except for the First Inhabitants…, a peaceable people among whom morbidity and mortality from RS is zero. Immunity from RS is extremely rare.

Research on the genetic and epigenetic consequences of RS is still short-term and inconclusive. Survivors – 0.05 per cent – are intensively studied and rehabilitated. Some are confined as a matter of public safety. Some choose to live in enclaves, such as the self-governing, self-supporting prison island of Quarm in the northern Deep and Dancing Ocean, whose culture is a stark reminder of our history.

A growing percentage of male survivors choose surgical castration, as testosterone is part of the complex biochemical constellation that triggers RS. The castrati…are now a thriving sub-culture.[21]

Universal Male Contraception, we are told involves an annual implant recognised by law:

Young men normally have the first implant on their fifteenth birthday, marked by a contraceptive stud…in the ear; the younger the man, the larger and more public the stud. Exemptions… include avowed celibates and homosexuals…some meta-gender people, and men who are sacramentally committed to fathering a child.[22]

Apart from these radical notions of the nature of violence and its link to male sexuality, Annie March's book explores what it would be like to live in a society in which the equilibrium and wellbeing of future generations is really a governing principle. In the years AE (Anthropocene Era) 7007-7010, the biosphere becomes critically endangered.

Key eco-systems…begin to collapse as a result of industrial pollution, rampant consumption, genetic engineering, over-population, electro-magnetic and nuclear radiation, war. Birth defects spike across all species. Robot- and cyber-wars turn upwards of a billion people into refugees.[23]

And in AE 7011-7014, the then unknown virus Redound Syndrome, explodes across the land:

Both enacted, wilful violence, and extreme intended violence, trigger perpetrator death by endocrine implosion within forty-eight hours. Three in ten men, two in twenty women, die.[24]

Famine, drought and natural disasters follow and the population falls by half, with a huge death toll from the coupling of war and Redound Syndrome. In AE 2018, two prophetic women "declare Year Zero…the Beginning of the End, the Great Choice, Hope," and this leads to a new Ecozoic Era. A peaceable Realm is inaugurated but all is not well, and so the story continues. It waits for you to read it and to experience, first-hand, as it were, a world that is so different to our own. It is almost everything our world is not, and it deeply challenges our presumptions and prejudices.

Other future worlds are described in Ursula K. Le Guin in her Hainish Cycle, which began in 1966 with *Rocannon's World*.[25] I have chosen four of these books because each explores a theme that relates to The Recovery of Love. The first is *The Left Hand of Darkness*,[26] which was first published in 1969; the second is *The Dispossessed*,[27] published in 1974; the third is *The Word for World is Forest*,[28] published in 1976; and the fourth is *The Telling*, published in 2000. [29]

Again and again, just as I have been imagining what I have taken to be new possibilities, I find that Ursula Le Guin has already done so. I had been asking questions about the possibility of an ungendered discourse, and then I read *The Left Hand of Darkness* in which the people of "the winter world of Gethen" are androgynous. Normally neuter, at the peak of their monthly sexual cycle they can become female or male. It is extraordinary that, fifty years ago, Ursula Le

Guin, a self-declared feminist, should be suggesting this as a future possibility, but she did. I found myself exploring the possibility of radical collaboration and then, in *The Dispossessed*, I found, in some distant future world, Annares, that women were treated equally with men in a society of collaboration and no ownership. At one point the main character, the scientist and mathematician Shevek, who comes from Anarres but gets to visit the world of Urras, explains to a revolutionary group of why he has come to them:

> I am here because you see in me the promise, the promise that we made two hundred years ago in this city – the promise kept. We have kept it, on Anarres. We have nothing but our freedom. We have nothing to give you but your own freedom. We have no law but the single principle of mutual aid between individuals. We have no government but the single principle of free association. We have no states, no nations, no presidents, no premiers, no chiefs, no generals, no bosses, no bankers, no landlords, no wages, no charity, no police, no soldiers, no wars. Nor do we have much else. We are sharers, not owners. We are not prosperous. None of us is rich. None of us is powerful. If it is Anarres you want, if it is the future you seek, then I tell you that you must come to it with empty hands. You must come to it alone, and naked, as the child comes into the world, into his future, without any past, without any property, wholly dependent on other people for his life. You cannot take what you have not given, and you must give yourself. You cannot buy the Revolution. You cannot make the Revolution. You can only be the Revolution. It is in your spirit, or it is nowhere.[30]

Then, as I explored the possibility of non-violence, I read *The Word for World is Forest*, and found that when the gentle Athsheans abandoned their long-held practice of violence, it endangered the very foundation of their society. And finally, in *The Telling*, we find, as I, too, have claimed, evidence of the damage of a corporatist, patriarchal, state, which controls language and reifies the economy, and the importance of a gentle and spiritual culture of story telling. I feel as if I have been exploring territory already mapped by this incredible person, Ursula K. Le Guin.

My point in reviewing the work of Starhawk, Annie March and Ursula K. Le Guin, women writing about the future – and especially Ursula Le Guin as the synchronicity here has been remarkable – is to claim that the transformation that I seek away from a narrow, controlling and damaging patriarchy is not mine alone, and that if we listen to the voices of women we find that they have imagined many intriguing possibilities. Indeed, they have proposed that the transformation they offer is both desirable and necessary for the continued flourishing of humankind.

Finally, then, one other woman's voice comes from a friend of mine, and fortunately for me my publisher, Lorna Howarth, and her co-author Genevieve Boast. And if the previous stories are about the distant future, this work is grounded in the present. Lorna is part of a group of women who, like the people of the Northlands in Starhawk's *The Fifth Sacred Thing*, meet regularly, as she says, to weave together the gifts of the elements – fire, air, earth and water – sharing wisdom on healthcare, child-care and earth-care, based on integrity, love, authenticity and friendship. Theirs is a way of being rooted in Nature. And Lorna says that although there needs to be a fruitful coming together of feminine and the masculine qualities:

> …we can't build authentic systems in a linear, male-dominated paradigm, we have to create them in reciprocity and trust… anyone – male or female or non-binary – who aspires to embody principles of love, respect, deep ecology, nurturing, joyfulness, ease and grace, is doing more to create Eden than they perhaps know.[31]

Somehow, for these women, it seems to be possible to create ways of being that depend on being in those ways. Lorna and Genevieve's book is titled *The Soulistic Journey*,[32] and subtitled, *A Pilgrimage to the Source of Your Being*; again, the emphasis here is on *being*, and the notion of 'pilgrimage' and a 'source of being' carry this work into a realm quite unlike the rather more academic debate of feminist essentialism and intersectionality. The women who follow the path described by Lorna and Genevieve, take their cue from Nature and

   Feminism and More

aspire to learn from Nature's intelligence, and when their book was complete, they gifted it to two hundred of their friends, family and colleagues. The book speaks of Solar (masculine) and Lunar (feminine) energies, of archetypal qualities, of Mystery (the shadow element) and Wisdom (the gift element), and of the seven directions of the Soulistic Wheel – North, South, East, West, Above, Below, and Within.[33] Each of these has a capital letter as they carry essence and meaning. With an awareness of our innate interdependence with Nature, the book speaks of the need for a new discourse in order to heal the ways in which we have become separated from Nature.

The authors acknowledge the sacred in all that is,[34] speaking of "a malaise at the heart of twenty-first century life,"[35] a malaise that arises from the presumption that "humanity is somehow more evolved, superior to or separate from the natural world... a belief that has given rise to devastation of ecosystems to such a degree that we are now compromising our own future."[36] And they say that it is this view of an anthropocentric representation of god that "diminishes our understanding of the Cosmos and the Universal laws to which we are all connected."[37] Their practice is to align their lives to the patterns and rhythms of Nature, and from this they and their companions draw solace.

This is work that requires great openness and sensitivity since Lorna says that whilst she and the women she works with are recovering and weaving their divine feminine energies, and in doing so bringing their deepest-held dreams into being – not least, the birthing of 'the New Earth' – there is still a sense that something is missing, which is expressed in questioning whether without the complementarity of evolved masculine energies, there may be the danger of the scales swinging out of balance once again in the opposite direction, to extreme matriarchy and all that may entail; and not only that, there will always be a sense of incompleteness. The whole, harmonious, balanced life impulse, say Lorna and Genevieve, is akin to the symbol of the caduceus staff: the entwining masculine and feminine energies embodied by the serpents, and the unifying, evolutionary energy symbolised by the wings.

And so, perhaps, whilst feminists agree that now is the time for their voices to be heard and for the scales to come back into balance, there will also come a time in the not-too-distant future when the evolved feminine and masculine unify into an 'ungendered whole' that marries the qualities of both, allows humanity to manifest its true, cosmological potential.

Of course, as an elderly man I have no more place in these gatherings of women than I do in the internal debates of feminism, in Starhawk's or Annie March's or Ursula Le Guin's world of imagination, or in Lorna Howarth's Loom, but above all else it seems to me that these women, and no doubt others like them, are opening the doors of possibility and widening the discussion of the ways in which, however we might call it, 'other' qualities might arise for us. They seem to include: collaboration, a care of the Earth, non-violence, nurture and healing, gender fluidity and an absence of a rigid and dominant hierarchy. Looking back to what I said in Chapter 2, I would say that these 'other' qualities can be found, can only be found, in the mysterious presence of Love. The many and varied forms of feminism and their more recent associations with marginalised and oppressed racial and other groups, accompanied as they are by queer theory, are much concerned with sex, sexuality and gender. They are of interest to me not only because of this, but also because, at their core, they question the definition of what is to be taken as 'normal', which, of course, brings us back to the matter of language that I discussed in Chapter 1 – to the constraints and damage of dominant forms of discourse.

Feminism and queer theory, in all their voices, are aligned with the question of that gendered discourse of which I spoke at the end of *Love and the Divine Feminine*. However, I need to take the exploration further for there is another – and I would say related – matter that I believe drives patriarchy. This is the matter of violence. In 2017, my colleague Scherto Gill, of the Guerrand-Hermès Foundation for Peace, and I edited a collection of essays titled *Peacefulness*.[38] The idea for the collection arose from a symposium we had attended which claimed to be about peace, but which, we felt, spoke only of conflict and violence, with peace as no more than a bandage to heal wounds, mostly after the event. I had asked Scherto whether it was possible to speak of peacefulness in and of itself, for itself. What do we know about peacefulness as a practice? The essays that we gathered and edited together were a first attempt to explore the expression and practice of peace in a variety of different settings including in economy, and in the Introduction we said:

> [This] book proposes that an appropriate understanding of peace cannot be limited to that which it is not. Indeed, such an understanding can only come about by appreciating and perceiving peace in and of itself, most especially through exploring peace not as something that is imposed from outside, but as a shared human aspiration, rooted in our innate peacefulness, and our relationship with others and within our communities and societies. When presenting peacefulness as connected to the state of being human, we are able to overcome the simplest division between inner and outer peace, and positive and negative peace.
>
> For these reasons, we suggest that peace and peacefulness be explored within three domains: first, within our state of being, as an aspect of spirituality; then in our relatedness, including communal relationships and social harmony; and, thirdly, in the public realm, including socio-economic systems, political structures, and global collaborations.[39]

But, however much we may have proposed such a notion, I remain shocked at the prevalence of violence, and most especially in our unquestioned assumptions about its necessary place in our communities and between nations. Global arms sales are something like three times the amount given in foreign aid.

I am not a scholar of these matters, but I have a deep sense that a significant cause of the oppression that people like Starhawk and Annie March and Ursula K. Le Guin talk about, is the problem of endemic violence, expressed not only in the violence of patriarchy towards women and towards those who have been marginalised, but, more generally, towards all of us and towards Nature. It astonishes me that despite all the evidence to the contrary, we continue to condone this violence, not least in forms of economy, in the language of 'takeover battles' and 'making a killing'. It may well be the case that crimes of violence have declined over long periods of time, but this only covers those acts of violence that we have deemed to be criminal. Within the all-pervasive culture of dominance, violence still persists and is still accepted as a necessary form of defence – and note that Starhawk, with all her ideas for non-violence, thought it would continue into the future. And yet, as the stories that we have looked at in this book suggest, accepting violence as 'just the way things are' is the same sort of unspoken prejudice as that towards people of another gender, sexuality race or religious belief.

I shall return to this later.

Endnotes

1. Alison Stone, *Essentialism and Anti-Essentialism in Feminist Philosophy*, eprints.lancs.ac.uk, 2004, 4.

2. Judith Butler, *Gender Trouble*, Routledge, 1990.

3. Ibid. 8.

4. Op cit, Alison Stone, 3.

5. Ibid. 15.

6. Ibid. 18.

7. Ibid. 24.

8. Ibid.

9. unwomen.org. 1st July 2020.

10. now.org. 'Feminism of the Future', posted 13th April 2013.

11. Judith Butler, *Gene Trouble*, Routledge, 2007, Preface (1999), xi to xxv.

12. Ibid. xxiv.

13. Starhawk.org.

14. Starhawk, *The Fifth Sacred Thing*, Bantam paperback, 1994.

15. I am not here suggesting that the Covid virus was

deliberately started and spread, but the presence of a pandemic is topical.

16.   Op cit, Starhawk, 1994, 17.

17.   Ibid.

18.   Ibid.

19.   Starhawk, *City of Refuge*, Califia Press, 2015.

20.   Annie March, *Butterfly's Children*, Panacea Books 2018.

21.   Ibid. 7.

22.   Ibid. 4-5.

23.   Ibid. 2.

24.   Ibid.

25.   Ursula K. Le Guin, *Rocannon's World*, Ace Books, 1966.

26.   Ursula K. Le Guin, *The Left Hand of Darkness*, Ace Books, 1969.

27.   Ursula K. Le Guin, *The Dispossessed*, Harper and Row, 1974.

28.   Ursula K. Le Guin, *The Word for World is Forest*, Berkley Books, 1976.

29.   Ursula K. Le Guin, *The Telling*, Ace Books, 2000.

30.   Ursula K. Le Guin, *The Dispossessed*, Gollancz, 2002, 248.

31.   Private correspondence.

32.	Genevieve Boast and Lorna Howarth, *The Soulisitic Journey*, Panacea Books, 2020.

33.	Ibid. 12.

34.	Ibid. 22.

35.	Ibid. 27.

36.	Ibid.

37.	Ibid.

38.	*Peacefulness: Being Peace and Making Peace*, Edited by David Cadman and Scherto Gill, Spirit of Humanity Press, 2017.

39.	Ibid. 8-9.

Introduction to Part Three

Those of us who wish to challenge the tyranny of patriarchy have the responsibility of offering alternative ways of being. Some of these have been heard in Part Two, in the voices of women, and now we come to some more 'pathways'. The first possibilities come from American scholars: the systems scientist and cultural historian Riane Eisler and the peace anthropologist Douglas P. Fry, and then the psychologist Kenneth Gergen. The second, introduces principles of Harmony, which arise from my work as Harmony Advisor to the Prince's Foundation, my role as Harmony Professor of Practice at the University of Wales Trinity St. David and my work with the Harmony in Education Project directed by my colleague Richard Dunne. The third possibility is the ancient Chinese teachings of The Tao and the I Ching, particularly The Tao with its teaching of movement from and to. And finally, given the dominance of what we might call The Economy – using capital letters to acknowledge its significance in our present culture – the last of the chapters in this part of the book represents some thoughts on an economy of Love. Now that would be something!

Chapter Seven

Partnerships and Relational Being

As the old patriarchal culture begins to break down, or at least, of necessity is being challenged more widely, new forms of discourse are being presented to us. We might say 'of course they are', because that is the way of things, the ever-present movement from and towards, the natural response to error and danger. But however that might be, examples of where we might be going to are needed and, fortunately, they exist. Two texts I have chosen by way of examples of this are Riane Eisler's and Douglas P. Fry's discussion of the shift from 'dominance' to 'partnership', and Kenneth Gergen's notions of 'relational being'. Each of these has to do with wholeness and connection, and each presents a challenge to the established and damaging discourse of separation, division and conflict.

In the late 1980s, the systems scientist and cultural historian, Riane Eisler, published a book called *The Chalice and the Blade*,[1] which explored the ways in which the cultures of goddesses were overtaken by cultures of gods, and then by a single male God, Yahweh. In the last chapter of this book, she introduced what she termed a new view of reality, *a movement away from dominance and towards partnership*. Thirty or so years later, and after further extensive thought and research, this time together with her co-author, the peace anthropologist, Douglas P. Fry, she took this theme forward into a book called *Nurturing Our Humanity*, with the subtitle of *How Domination and Partnership Shape Our Brains, Lives and Futures*.[2] Again, this is a book with a long reach back into the evolutionary development of humankind, and it describes both a path taken and one that may be taken.

The key message of the new book is that the cultures that replaced the world of the goddesses were cultures of conquest and conflict, cultures in which the good of the people was thought to rest in the dominance of the few, nearly all of whom were men, and beset with rigid hierarchies and rankings. Eventually, these forms

   Partnerships and Relational Being

of dominance became so hard-wired into our brains that they were seldom questioned. Nevertheless, pointing to recent knowledge coming from neuroscience, the authors say that it is now understood that domination-oriented societies are extremely stressful, and that stress can inhibit our capacity for empathy and mutuality:

> [Stress] stems from the conflation of caring and coercion built into domination childrearing, leading to denial (including identification with the 'strong') and deflection of fear and rage to out-groups. The socialization of males to equate masculinity with domination and violence is still another source of stress, as is the attendant devaluation of anything stereotypically associated with 'inferior' women (such as caring, caregiving, and non-violence). All this manifests itself in the development of neural structures primed for fight, flight or freeze, which promote fear and denial, suppress empathy, and constrict consciousness of a partnership alternative.[3]

Domination cultures are also socially conditioned:

> Once we connect the dots, we see that in a domination system, familial, educational, religious, political, and economic structures – *not* an imagined human nature wired for oppression and violence – are what gets in the way of our human capacities, indeed, propensities, for empathy, caring, and mutuality.[4]

In contrast to the established culture of dominance, the authors propose a culture of partnership. Whilst the components of the former are, hierarchy, ranking, the cultural acceptance of abuse and violence, and the belief that the rankings of dominance are inevitable, the components of the latter are an egalitarian structure, an equal partnership between women and men, a cultural rejection of abuse and violence, and a belief in human nature as being about empathy, and mutual respect.[5] In the culture of partnership, typical human relations are seen as based upon precepts geared towards the social good rather than upon a narrow, more selfish, unjust and conflictual individual good.

The authors suggest that such partnership societies flourished for millennia before the culture of dominance overwhelmed them and that they are, therefore, closer to our natural way of being. Indeed, they suggest that they are an expression of the long evolution of humankind: "the movement towards a more partnership-oriented world has not failed – rather it is incomplete."[6]

In clearing up misperceptions about the differences between 'dominance' and 'partnership', they highlight the following: whilst both types of culture may enjoy co-operation, the difference lies in their purpose, with teamwork in partnership cultures being concerned with human wellbeing and reciprocity rather than being harnessed to some form of exploitation; whilst both cultures may at times work within hierarchies, those in partnership cultures seek to empower not dominate; whilst competition may be present in either culture, it is less overt in partnership cultures, which are more concerned with excellence than supremacy; and whilst both cultural systems will experience conflict, in partnership cultures it will be used to facilitate creative solutions rather than division and antagonism.

And then, and it is one aspect of these proposals that I find to be of particular interest, the authors say that "with a movement towards the partnership side of the continuum, rigid gender stereotypes have begun to melt away."[7] In such cultures, for example in Finland, they say, gender roles are flexible, whereas "in domination systems they are rigid, with the devaluation of women and the 'feminine'."[8]

So, in terms of my quest for an ungendered discourse, it would seem that in this 'other language' of partnership we can see a movement away from what is regarded as the masculine towards the feminine, and in this an inclination towards integration, collaboration and a care of one another. Or, to put it the other way round, it is these very qualities that are required for a culture of partnership. And, again of interest to me, the authors make it clear that the energy flowing through these qualities, and through this possible transformation, is the lost quality of Love. Echoing the underlying proposition of this book, the authors of *Nurturing Our Humanity* say that in partnership both Love and

   Partnerships and Relational Being

the Feminine are recovered by what they call "our human need and capacity for love."[9]

The feelings, motivations and behaviours we call love have deep evolutionary roots. Indeed, these roots go back millions of years before our species emerged… because immature mammals require care to survive.[10]

Love, say the authors, "is a dynamic that helps *explain* the emergence of humanity…[and] the emergence of our species would not have been possible without the emergence of caring and love."[11] This quality of love is made possible by our larger and more complex brains. Indeed, "the evolution of this large, more complex brain may not have been possible were it not for the evolutionary movement toward nurturing love."[12] Or perhaps, to echo the title of this book, 'The Recovery of Love', there is the suggestion that there is a connection between Love and the Feminine, for apparently in the Democratic Republic of the Congo live the bonobos, a primate closely related to humans. Unlike its other close relation, the chimpanzee, bonobos do not have a male-dominated social structure, "and their social relations are much more geared toward sharing and caring."[13] Interestingly, the bonobos' use sex "as a means reinforcing social relations based on the give-and-take of shared pleasure rather than on coercion and fear."[14] Dominance does not enter into their sexual activity.

Bonobo society is not male-dominated. Females, particularly mothers, play key social roles. Bonobo males do not use sexual coercion against females, and female bonobos form strong social bonds and effectively cooperate to keep male aggression down.[15]

Now there's a thing!

And so it is that an alternative evolutionary perspective emerges, one in which the first social bonds arise not from fear but between mothers and infants based on sharing and caring as the foundation for social bonds in later life. This offers us the possibility of "a more gender-balanced evolutionary narrative,"[17] which the authors relate to archaeological findings that suggest the importance of women in the Palaeolithic or Old Stone Age:

> Evidence for this new, more balanced evolutionary story has been accumulating in recent years. For example, archaeological finds point to the importance of women in the Palaeolithic or Old Stone Age. The majority of stone carvings of this era are female figurines. And a recent analysis of the handprints sometimes found on the walls of famous cave sanctuaries show that the majority were female hands.[18]

And:

> In the early Neolithic, too, female figurines are ubiquitous – until they rather abruptly disappear. Yet even after this cultural shift, female deities were still prominent. For example, the Egyptian goddess Isis was revered as a dispenser of wisdom, counsel, and justice, and in ancient Sumer the most widely worship deity was Inanna, the Goddess of Love.[19]

And then, at the end of their chapter titled 'Love, the Brain and Becoming Human', the authors say this:

> Without love – given and received – our lives would feel diminished in meaning. This deep human need for meaning is another motivation that cannot be explained in terms of the replication of genes or even by our sexual drive.
>
> However, when it comes to the crucial question of whether our needs for meaning and love are met and whether our capacities for creativity and love are expressed or inhibited [...] we need to consider whether a society orients to the partnership or domination end of the continuum.[20]

Later, you may not be surprised to note, they conclude not only that our capacities for creativity and love are best served in partnership, but that domination causes real damage:

The culture into which the child is born makes a huge difference… Families in domination systems typically are authoritarian and male-dominated, with stressful and punitive childrearing. [And] the damage done by this kind of childrearing goes further because children are taught that rankings of domination are normal and that they must submit to those in control.[21]

Given my exploration of the Feminine, it is of interest to read that studies have shown that whilst we respond to stress in three basic ways – fight-or-flight, dissociation and tend-or-befriend – each of these activates different neuro-chemical patterns and behaviours, and it is said that women cope with stress in their own way, frequently "by joining together to care for one another and for their own and others' children."[22] Studies have shown that "the tend-or-befriend response involves oxytocin, vasopressin and other substances connected with bonding, caring, and caregiving."[23] This tend-or-befriend response is clearly a form of partnering rather than domination, and it would seem that it may be ancient in its origin.

For the purpose of this chapter, what I draw from Riane Eisler's and Douglas P. Fry's work is this: the assurance that love and nurture are part of being; that we have much to learn of this from women and from the feminine mode of being; that there is 'another future', one based upon collaboration and partnership; and that as we evolve we can leave, we are meant to leave, dominance behind us.

I was introduced to Kenneth Gergen and his book *Relational Being*,[24] by my colleague Scherto Gill, and soon I found myself in a Zoom call with an elderly man, well someone like me, sitting in his study in America. I liked him at once, and I began to listen to what he had to say. It's quite important.

Like many great truths, it seems obvious when you hear it – of course, it must be so. For what Kenneth Gergen writes about is the evident truth that despite what we may have been told, we are never single, we are always part of. We can never be entirely separate. It just isn't possible.

As historians report, the view of the individual as singular and separate, one whose abilities to think and feel are central to life, and whose capacity for voluntary action is prized, is of recent origin. It is a conception of human nature that took root only four centuries ago, during a period that we now view as the Enlightenment. It was during this period that the soul or spirit, as the central ingredient of being human, was largely replaced by individual reason.[25]

My attempt, he says:

is to generate an account of human action that can replace the presumption of bounded selves with a vision of relationship. I do not mean relationships between otherwise separate selves, but rather, a process of coordination that precedes the very concept of the self... We are always already emerging from relationship; we cannot step out of relationship; even in our most private moments we are never alone... [And] the future well-being of the planet depends significantly on the extent to which we can nourish and protect not individuals, or even groups, but the generative process of relating.[26]

According to Kenneth Gergen,[27] the words "always already emerging from relationship" are borrowed from Heidegger, and now circulate across academia as a way of pointing to an invariable, or grounding presence from which our actions emerge. It's to say, in this case, that our immersion in relational process is always and already there in the moment we act. Or, to put it another way, we cannot step out of the process without stepping out of humanity. He, therefore, invites us to move beyond cause and effect in understanding relationships and to "consider the world in terms of relational confluence."[28] In our troubled time, this is a radical, vital and heretical proposition. To place the individual always within relationship with others, is to deny the dominant doctrine of individuality and separation. But given where that doctrine has taken us, it is necessary to say this, and refreshing to hear it said. For in using the word 'being' rather than 'self' we are asked to move beyond the constricted noun into the more fluid realm of verbs:

> In being, we are in motion, carrying with us a past as we move through the present into becoming.[29]

Citing Wittgenstein's account of the origins of meaning in language (language game theory) wherein the meanings of words are derived from their application within social relations, Kenneth Gergen challenges the intellectual tradition of individualism in which the self is conceived as an atomic, autonomous entity of bounded being, and suggests that independent persons do not form a relationship by coming together; rather, it is through the process of collaborative action (what he coins as *co-action*) that the potentiality for independent persons can emerge – "the individual represents the common intersection of myriad relationships".[30] In other words, we do not possess emotions, thoughts and self-awareness independent of relationships; rather it is because we participate in relational traditions that we recognize ourselves as having emotions, thoughts and a sense of self, offering the framework through which one can navigate and negotiate when, where, and how this sense of self can be performed. The self is constituted by a confluence of performative relationships, situated and constantly re-situated within new environments and contexts, both social and extra-social. As such, Kenneth Gergen's concept of the self defies the tendency towards abstraction; it is ineluctably mediated by relational materiality. Thus, he writes:

> The word 'I' does not index an origin of action, but a relational achievement.[31]

For Kenneth Gergen, then, all intelligible actions are *relational in origin and performance*. Isolated actions in themselves do not carry meaning. Even our most private and solitary moments are always immersed in relational actions, operating within a social framework which prioritizes mutual interconnectedness and interrelatedness. Thus, he summarizes that "to be a person is not to exist in a fundamental state of freedom, but of constraint,"[32] the constraint of always being in relationship with the other. The very emerging into the world is an emergence into social, *relational* being; the first caress of our mothers forever casts us into webs of relational motion specified and respecified by soft, dynamic, ever-changing constraints described as a "vitalizing enchainment."[33] And this motion can be understood as a multidirectional process of *relational flow* marked by simultaneous "movement towards constraint, on the one hand, and an openness to the evolution of meaning on the other." [34]

One of the primary issues he identifies with the dominant ideology of bounded being is the primacy it places upon the closed self and its development as a fundamentally separate unit. Such a linear rationalization of the individual, he suggests, is symptomatic of broader tendencies towards the categoric separation of phenomena, people and concepts: "in a world of cause and effect, everyone clamours to be a cause."[35] Thus the individualism of bounded being pervades the ideological structures which undergird our economic, political and social systems. Just so, say I.

As such, this critique presented through the concept of relational being is a basis for the practical application of relationality within society, from the level of personal relationships to broader political schema. We are presented with a worldview that goes beyond the identification of separable and dichotomized units – he-versus-she, I-versus-you, us-versus-them – and instead, we are asked to consider an understanding of meaning itself as co-created, where social reality is constituted fundamentally by *relatedness*. Each person is now a part of the 'we', or what Kenneth Gergen terms a 'multi-being'; each person is embedded in an emergent web of continuously reiterating relational processes embodied through performance and action. In other words, the focus shifts from the individual dancers to the dance; from the 'essence' to the 'way';[36] from the individual musicians to the music-making. Furthermore, this proposition distinguishes between two types of relational process – those which are generative and those which are degenerative.[37] While the former is catalytic, capable of injecting relations with creative vitality, the latter is corrosive, bringing co-action to an end, and moving towards a "condition of alienation,"[38] most notably present in our dominant economic theory and practice where:

> [the] tradition of bounded being carries far beyond the daily experience of self and others. It is also realized in our ways of life and the structures of our institutions – schools, businesses, and democracy itself.[39]

And, in these ways:

> [as] the father of economic theory, Adam Smith characterized human action, it is essentially based upon self-interest... [and here] a calculus of self-gratification is [seen as being] central to all human action.[40]

According to this view, even human love is a matter of making a profit, all values are abandoned save market values. Economic interests are pursued to the exclusion of all else, and the "longstanding and much cherished tradition of the individual self carries with it enormous costs."[41]

It is therefore useful, says Kenneth Gergen, to envision forms of generative process, those in which new and enriching potentials are opened through the flow of interchange.[42] His hope is that we might, "recast the discourse of the mind in such a way that human connection replaces separation as the fundamental reality."[43] And this is the task towards which I am drawn in this book, for it seems to me that without developing and adopting a relational discourse such as this, we cannot even begin to tackle the present damage and potential catastrophe of our present lives, our present ways of being.

Endnotes

1. Riane Eisler, *The Chalice and the Blade*, Harper and Row, paperback edition, 1988.

2. Riane Eisler and Douglas P. Fry, *Nurturing Our Humanity: How Domination and Partnership Shape Our Brains, Lives and Futures*, Oxford University Press, 2019.

3. Ibid. 33.

4. Ibid. 35.

5. Ibid. 99-100.

6. Ibid. 101.

7. Ibid. 104.

8. Ibid.

9. Ibid. 44.

10. Ibid. 47.

11. Ibid. 49.

12. Ibid. 50.

13. Ibid. 56.

14. Ibid. 57.

15. Ibid. 58.

Partnerships and Relational Being

16.   Ibid. 59.

17.   Ibid. 60.

18.   Ibid. 60.

19.   Ibid.

20.   Ibid. 61.

21.   Ibid. 80.

22.   Ibid. 81.

23.   Ibid.

24.   Kenneth Gergen, *Relational Being: Beyond Self and Community*, Oxford University Press, 2011.

25.   Ibid. xiv.

26.   Ibid. xv.

27.   Private correspondence, November, 2021.

28.   Op cit, Kenneth Gergen, xvi

29.   Ibid. xxvi.

30.   Ibid. 150.

31.   Ibid. 133.

32.   Ibid. 40.

33.   Ibid.

34.   Ibid. 46.

35.   Ibid. 51.

36.   See Hall, David L., and Roger T. Ames. *Thinking from the Han: Self, Truth, and Transcendence in Chinese and Western Culture*. Albany, New York, 1998.

37.   Op cit, Kenneth Gergen, 47.

38.   Ibid.

39.   Ibid. 20.

40.   Ibid. 21.

41.   Ibid. 27.

42.   Ibid. 47.

43.   Ibid. 62.

CHAPTER EIGHT

Principles of Harmony

In the last chapter, we looked at two pathways that might lead us towards 'another language', the pathways of 'partnership' and 'relational being'. Another such pathway is provided by the notion of Harmony, and this pathway is being explored in a variety of places, including the University of Wales Trinity Saint David's Harmony Institute of which I am an Associate. *The Harmony Debates*,[1] is a collection of essays collected together by Nick Campion, the Director of the Institute, and in this collection, I contributed a short text which set out some possible Harmony principles, which relate to Riane Eisler's and Douglas P. Fry's notions of partnership and to Kenneth Gergen's relational being.

In my text on Harmony principles, I said this:

My proposition is this: it would seem that all human societies seek to describe their relationships with each other, and with that of which they feel themselves to be part, in terms of some kind of order, a set of relationships which govern them, and one attempt to do this is to speak of harmony, and within this task one attempt is to look at harmony as it is expressed in Nature to try and discern Nature's principles of harmony.

Within Nature there are a number of characteristic qualities or principles that speak of harmony. I say a number, but by that I do not mean to presume that the number is limited by that which I have observed. That is why I speak of principles of harmony and not of *the* principles of harmony. I do not presume to have discovered the defining set of principles, only to have observed what I take to be some of those principles. Nature is more wonderful than we can possibly imagine. The principles I have observed include wholeness, connection, interdependence, diversity within wholeness, cycles of time and season, patterns, rhythms, reciprocity and mutuality and justice and lawfulness, and I accept that what I have found may have been what I was looking for and others would find something else.

Nevertheless, what I have seen suggests a systemic order of intertwined and entangled patterns of rhythms that might constitute a from of governance that, if followed, would align with that which is good for us and good for the Earth; and I

     Principles of Harmony

propose this not simply by way of detached intellectual enquiry but also by way of experience, by practice and participation. For I find that when I live as if my life is ordered by harmony, harmonious relationships are inclined to manifest, and this must surely be so for, as the Buddha made clear in the opening stanza of the Dhammapada, it is with our thoughts that we make the world. And in my own work I claim that the governing principle of this order is Love.[2]

As Nicholas Campion said in his Introduction to *The Harmony Debates*, Harmony is an overarching philosophy which seeks to provide a broad guide for action:

The idea of harmony as balance and order can be traced back to the classical Greek world, where *harmonia* meant 'union' or 'fitting together'. And it was the Greek philosophers who articulated the concept, widespread in the ancient world, that the entire universe is a single integrated whole. The movement of the stars and planets, they believed, make sounds as they travel and, if we could hear these, they would make a beautiful melody. This is the foundation of the 'Harmony of the Spheres', a notion which was popular amongst Renaissance thinkers and inspired a belief that the purpose of culture, politics and religion should be to avoid conflict and manage collective affairs for the benefit of all. The same ideas about universal balance and the integration of all things occur in many cultures in multiple forms.

The worldviews which maintain this notion are well established. They include Stoicism from the classical Greek and Roman world, Buddhism from India, and Taoism and Confucianism from China. The belief that all things are related also pervades traditional and indigenous cultures. All these ways of thinking and living are alive and influential in the modern world and have much to say about our relationship with the environment and politics.[3]

But let me take a step back and look at another source. For some years, I was first the co-editor and then the editor of a collection of the speeches and articles of His Royal Highness The Prince of Wales, published in three bound volumes. At the core of this work was the matter of Harmony, for more than anything else, The Prince of Wales has proposed, and led the way in proposing, the need for a more harmonious relationship between humankind and Nature, and the need for greater understanding and tolerance, greater harmony, between and amongst each one of us.

At the root of The Prince's expression and practice of Harmony has been 'sacred geometry', and this notion of proportion and order as a universal and timeless principle has for many years been taught at his Foundation's School of Traditional Arts, which studies the arts and crafts of the great traditions, not least the Islamic tradition.

In a text prepared for the third volume of the *Speeches and Articles* archive, The Prince said this:

> I have gained a great deal of insight into the meaning of Islamic symbolism and of the universal geometry that constitutes the grammar of harmony from the renowned world authority on sacred architecture, [the late] Professor Keith Critchlow, who helped me found and direct my School of Traditional Arts in London some twenty years ago. An architect himself, he has dedicated his life to the study of the ancient principles and how they work in sacred buildings. He told me once a wonderful old Chinese story about an ancient sage who was asked by his young pupil to draw a picture of the universe. The old man hardly hesitated before picking up his brush and promptly making three swift strokes on the page. First he drew a circle, below it a triangle, and below them both a square.[5]

The circle, the triangle and the square, when combined together are the foundation of the great cathedrals, mosques and temples and their proportions are present in the patterning and spiral of Nature, they are revealed in the proportions of the Golden Mean, the Fibonacci Ratios, and the scales of music.

Again in this text, The Prince said:

> On the mathematical level this is all very interesting, perhaps it is even entertaining, but my point is that, wherever it appears, we find this shaping and patterning so naturally pleasing. Whether it be the shape of a plant, the arrangement of petals in a flower or the harmonies of the music made when it is constructed according to this numerical relationship, we call it 'beautiful'; we have a sense of an immeasurable quality; we feel something special and indefinable when these numbers are at play. There are even well-documented experiments where different groups of people have been shown pictures of different faces and asked individually to say which ones they find more beautiful and, generally, they tend to settle on those images where a person's features conform most readily to the ratio of the Golden Section – the relationship, for example, between the width of the eyes and the length of the nose, or the width of the mouth to the width and height of the forehead; even the spacing of the teeth. It seems that we resonate naturally with the proportions that reflect this golden proportion. No wonder the banks decided that credit cards should be golden mean rectangles or that Apple decided to use this ratio to create the shape of its first iPod.[6]

And again, he said:

> The Grammar of Harmony is therefore the grammar that underpins the structure and growth of all things in the natural world, and we resonate with these patterns because they are our patterns too – we are made up of them, just as every tree, plant and flower is made up of them..[7]

So, when The Prince of Wales talks about Harmony he is talking about a universal and timeless informing principle that shapes all that is good, and whose absence in our lives is harmful.

One of the most moving and powerful texts of the first two volumes of the archive of his speeches and articles is an article published in the *Temenos Academy Review* in Autumn 2002. The article was titled "A Time to Heal" and at the very end, The Prince wrote this:

As I have grown older I have gradually come to realize that my entire life, so far, has been motivated by a desire to heal: to heal the dismembered landscape and the poisoned soil; the cruelly shattered townscape, where harmony has been replaced by cacophony; to heal the divisions between intuitive and rational thought, between mind, body and soul so that the example of our humanity can once again be lit by a sacred flame; to level the monstrous barrier erected between Tradition and Modernity; and, above all, to heal the mortally wounded soul that, alone, can give us warning of the folly of playing God and believing that knowledge on its own is a substitute for wisdom.[8]

Harmony and healing come together. In our Introduction to Volumes 1 and 2 Professor Bushrui and I referred to the work that The Prince has undertaken in the light of Harmony as follows:

[This] is a story about a young prince, brought up with a deep sense of duty and the need to match words with action. This is a prince who in his teenage years, becomes distressed by what he sees as a deliberate attempt not only to separate present from past, but to abandon the principles and meaning of a timeless tradition – in his own words, to 'throw out the baby with the bathwater'. The 'tradition' in question is not a longing for the past or a crude sentimentality: it is a golden thread of wisdom that speaks of balance, order and connection, and of a reverence for Nature as a whole, something that is sacred. It is, therefore, a living tradition.

As he grows in experience and understanding, this prince comes to see that what at first seem to be things separate and apart are, in fact, aspects of a single whole. Intuitively, and with study, he comes to see that there are systemic principles at work, which we ignore at our peril. Most especially, in all that is going wrong, he sees the absence of the single principle of Harmony. And it is this principle, together with his innate sense of the greater need for action and not words, that leads him to inspire and establish organizations that work tirelessly for the individual-in-community; often for those whose voice is not heard – young people in inner-city areas, people of faith, local communities wanting to have a say in their own redevelopment, small farmers and shopkeepers, teachers wanting to teach their subject with passion and depth, those in healthcare who see that there might be a better integration of traditional and mainstream medicine and care. And, most recently, this is a prince who, seeing Nature as a whole and as a living system, is prepared to urge us to consider more carefully not only the ways in which we farm and fish and forest, but also the ways in which we shop and consume the goods of the Earth.[9]

And as he has put it himself in the text prepared for the third Volume of the archive:

This is why I have long tried to remind people that the Grammar of Harmony is not some irrelevant, nebulous scheme, nor an engaging way of describing an approach to design that somehow, in some long since passed Golden Age, people suddenly came up with in order to create some of the most astonishing works of art and architecture in all of history. No. The Grammar of Nature's Harmony is the foundation of the language by which we may properly understand how the world works and see it for what it really is. It is joined up, all one thing, profoundly interdependent and, by a recognition of its limits, ultimately self-sustaining.[10]

So, then, we can see that for The Prince of Wales Harmony is no small thing. And, in all of this (and kin to the matters of language that I raised in Chapter 1), a key feature of The Prince's work has been his understanding of what he has described as 'a crisis of perception'. He suggests that the difficulties we face – climate breakdown, the erosion of resources, extreme poverty and even an unstable economy

– arise not from technical glitches, but in a crisis founded in the very values and principles that knowingly or not shape how we see, understand and experience the world. This radical claim, he says, goes to the root of our present concern with economic, social and environmental sustainability. [11]

The Prince finds the root cause of our present crises arises from an imbalance – a loss of Harmony – brought about by the dogma of post-war Modernism which, no doubt with good intent and with the aim of improving our material wellbeing, has ignored the limits of Nature, the need to see ourselves as 'part of' and not 'apart from' Nature. Restoring balance, restoring harmony, healing our relationship with Nature, informs all of his work. Increasingly over recent years, he has spoken of the relationship between the environment, society and the economy, and he has, for a long time, pointed to an underlying crisis of values, challenging the common convention of selfishness and greed which shapes notions of thoughtless economic growth, unlimited consumption and financial speculation. Indeed, in his message to the COP21 gathering in Paris in December 2015, he said:

> On an increasingly crowded planet, humanity faces many threats – but none is greater than climate change. It magnifies every hazard and tension of our existence. It threatens our ability to feed ourselves; to remain healthy and safe from extreme weather; to manage the natural resources that support our economies, and to avert the humanitarian disaster of mass migration and increasing conflict.[12]

So, it would seem that in tackling climate change and resource depletion, including the social and economic consequences that arise therefrom, and indeed in addressing the whole matter of social, economic and environmental sustainability, The Prince of Wales proposes that in order to clarify our perception we must first understand and align ourselves with principles of Harmony.

Principles of Harmony

Leaving aside for the moment what The Prince has said, and turning to my own work, in this book I want to explore this 'crisis of perception' a bit more deeply. And in this, and in speaking of the links between economy, environment and society, I must, of course, stress that I am speaking for myself and not for The Prince of Wales – although, as I have said, he has for many years made clear that there are direct links between, for example, businesses and the environment and businesses and community.

In Buddhist teachings, perception, or *sañña*, is very important. It is one of the five aggregates (*skandhas*) by which we make sense of the world – form, sensation, perception, mental formations and consciousness. The teaching is that to become enlightened we must first see things as they truly are, since perception shapes thoughts, which shape action. Indeed, as I have already said, in the opening stanza of the *Dhammapada*, the Buddha says that the way in which we see the world becomes concrete in the world.

This teaching is part of a long, but sometimes forgotten, tradition. If we were sitting here in the twelfth and thirteenth centuries, our perception would no doubt be governed by a theological view of the world, a view dominated and managed by the teachings and authority of the Church. We would most likely take as given that all that happens is shaped by this – markets, scholarship, society and so on, all shaped by a theological imperative.

As I suggested in Chapter 1, today we are now governed by another dominant worldview. We don't call it Theology, we call it Economy, or more particularly the Liberal Market Economy. But we, too, have priests. We call them businessmen and bankers. And the world they profess is not only one in which the so-called rules of their world are assumed to prevail, but also one in which to question them is heresy. This is a world of money, pricing and debt, of low levels of financial regulation and a dogma that proposes that the greatest good arises from growing the economy without limit. To play our part in this we must consume and then consume more, if necessary borrowing to be able to do so. For unless we do this, how can the economy grow? This is a world in which one Vice Chancellor in the UK told a gathering of departmental professors that they had to 'sweat their assets'; a world in which one distressed nurse in an American hospital described as 'a crisis' having given treatment to a man who had failed to disclose that he had no health insurance. This is a world where efficiency is described in financial terms and where the education of children is dominated by their potential economic value. This is also a world in which unregulated commerce, for example in fishing, forestry and the mining of coal and oil, has created a climatic crisis of severe proportions. This is a world at odds with the principles of balance and order expressed in Harmony.

Challenging such a dominant worldview is difficult, not least because, as in the twelfth and thirteenth centuries, its governing propositions are deeply embedded and taken for granted. We live our lives shaped by these propositions but are often unaware of them. So it is that in almost any conversation about how we should proceed someone is bound to say: 'We must be more business-like'. Or in any proposed conference or in the forming of any committee, someone will say: 'We must have someone who understands business'. And yet, the odd thing is that it is these very businesses and being business-like, that has brought upon us the impending crises of resource depletion and climate collapse, and, in so doing has created a world in which the gap between the rich and the poor has become ever wider, creating what an increasing number of observers say is a dangerous social and economic instability. Not trickle down but trickle up! Although I recognise that it is heresy to say so, perhaps we should be less business-like!

In my own work, for example in my work with the Spirit of Humanity Forum, and with the Guerrand Hermès Foundation for Peace – in a book entitled *Why Love Matters: Values in Governance*[13] – and in my own writings, I have proposed another root principle, the principle of Love. As we have seen in Chapter 2, my proposition is that all that is, when it is most true, is an expression of, and is shaped

    Principles of Harmony

by, the energetic force of Love. Love is of the essence, and we should align ourselves to Love in all that we do, both in our private and our public lives. Love is true and harmonious.

As we shall see, I have brought this root principle to the matter of economics and have argued that there are no absolute forms of economy, only different economies shaped by different underlying values, so that, if you wish to question or challenge any particular form of economy, such as ours, you should look to question and challenge its core values. And if we seek to construct another kind of economy, we needs must ensure that it is in accord with our own root principles. Otherwise, we live in a tyranny and should say so.

But there is something that happens before all of this, which is vital to an understanding of Harmony – and here I want to refer to work of the scholar Joseph Milne, who is a theologian, a philosopher and a Fellow of the Temenos Academy. He is important because more than anyone else I know he provides us with a perception of wholeness and interconnection that pre-dates the Enlightenment, a perception that has been lost, but which is utterly relevant to the present day. He has written many texts and given many lectures, but the two texts that I want to refer to here are *Metaphysics and the Cosmic Order* [14] and *The Mystical Cosmos*.[15] The first of these is important because it provides a description of three levels of knowing: the Religious, the Philosophical and the Empirical. Each of these plays its part in the matter of knowing, but each is separate:

It will be helpful to clarify these three levels. By the Religious I mean the revelatory, sacred Presence in all things, the disclosure of the created realm as an act within the mind of God. ... From this level come all the various 'sacred cosmologies' that are symbolic articulations of the divine ground of all that exists.

By the Philosophical I mean the metaphysical understandings or contemplation of the essence of reality...

...By the Empirical I mean the entire realm of observational and inferential deduction of the laws and nature of visible reality, the realm of the empirical sciences, of 'objective' knowledge...[16]

Whilst each of these levels of knowing has its part to play, they should not be mistaken for each other. For example, if I have a toothache I must go to a dentist, someone who has an empirical understanding of the nature of teeth. If, on the other hand, I want to understand the meaning of suffering in the human condition, it is unlikely that the dentist will help me. Rather I need a philosopher or a theologian. In our time, empiricism has all but expunged the theological and the philosophical, and in so doing has sought to explain the world to us in a language that is insufficient to the task.

An important part of this shortcoming is the manner in which we are supposed to know. The modern, scientific, and therefore empirical, definition of knowing is based upon sensory perception and calculation. As Joseph Milne puts it, such knowing would not have been regarded as knowledge for Plato and Aristotle:

For them knowledge of the cosmos was not for the sake of explanation or for accounting for everything in a single system or model. Their enquiries into reality are not a prelude to modern scientific enquiry as has often been claimed. Their concern for the truth of things is a fundamentally different kind of concern, and it therefore opens up an entirely different order of reality, an order completely passed over in the Age of Reason and the Enlightenment. For Plato and Aristotle the pursuit of truth is understood as adequate response to the Real, a coming into a right relationship with what most truly is.[17]

This then brings us into another "disposition towards reality,"[19] a realm not of objectification, but of, please note, *relationship*, a realm of *being* and a quest not for separation, but for *union*:

From the ancient Greek philosophers to Aquinas in the late Middle Ages it was understood that a relation exists between the human mind and the nature of things.[19]

And:

The being or presentness of things is not like our modern notion

Principles of Harmony

of 'fact'. The facts of things are secondary and often transitory. What Aristotle is observing is that what first presents itself to the intelligence is Being, not features or characteristics or qualities, and that all else that might be known of things follows only after Being.[20]

In this sense, the primary question is not what can we know, but *how shall we be*.

This is not the place to take this further, but I would urge you to read what Joseph Milne has to say. And I would also ask you to consider that what it suggests is this: how we perceive matters, because we shall only find what we perceive, and the manner of our perception will become manifest. And furthermore, it suggests that at a time of 'crisis' when we can see before us the consequences of actions based upon the exclusive dogma of empiricism, we might well ask ourselves whether or not there are other ways of 'seeing' that are natural to us and that are required to enable us to act wisely.

Finally, there is this. Those who have studied these things say that we are shaped by the stories we tell each other and by the stories that are told to us. If this is so, then we have to look carefully at these stories and if we find them unsatisfactory, we need to find others. For if we continue to tell stories that are not true we will lose our way. In a way, this is what The Prince of Wales has been trying to do for over forty years. Sensing that Modernism was too strident and was in danger, as we have heard him say, of 'throwing out the baby with the bathwater', he has asked us to take account of stories that are wise and timeless.

One of these stories is of Aphrodite and the birth of Harmony. Arising, it is said, from the waters of Love, and brought forth twixt the seasons and the winds, the beautiful Aphrodite, gives birth to a daughter, Harmonia – gives birth to renewal, harmony, balance and order. And so it is that each year, Beauty arises from Love, and carries the possibility of renewal and harmony. It is there in everything we see as the year turns. It arises from the cold darkness of Earth and Winter. It is born into the growing light of Spring. Its coming to be is there in the magical transformation of life that takes place in the dark time, to which, one day, all will return. This is eternal Harmony, beautiful, true and good, without which nothing can be.

But we cannot just assume that all will be well. For, as the story tells us, united with Ares, the god of war, Aphrodite also gives birth to two other children, Phobos (Fear) and Deimos (Terror). Whilst, therefore, this union brings harmony, it also bears with it the possibility of dis-harmony, the possibility of that fearfulness which is the enemy of Love. Indeed, the story tells us that unless we act with wisdom and with a pure heart, there is every possibility that all will not be well; that unless we have courage and overcome our hubris the possibility of catastrophe is real and ever-present. Disruptive forces, such as greed and fear are ever-present possibilities, manifest in the realms of Nature, Economy and Society.

So, we should not be surprised when storm, flood, pestilence and financial disruption arise from acts based upon greed and selfishness – when, instead of seeking to sustain, we seek short-term gain and a narrow and self-regarding gratification. Markets and communities can work in tune with each other or not; but to bring wellbeing they have to work both within their own realm and within a broader set of loving relationships between the social, the economic and the environmental. When we act otherwise, we are likely to come across Phobos and Deimos. For the story of Aphrodite tells us that if we want to nurture and sustain, we need to choose Love not Fear. Love matters. Love opens up and brings together, but Fear works to close down the possibility of change. Therefore, at a time (such as now) when significant change is required, Fear will be the enemy; it will hold us back and tempt us to hold onto 'business as usual'; it will constrain what we may take to be possible instead of enabling us to move; it will make us hesitate and shrink back. And wherever Fear is present, there is a lessening of trust, the very quality needed if we are to move towards more understanding and co-operation.

We might now call this necessary integration of the economic, the social and environmental, 'sustainability' – but when we

    Principles of Harmony

do, we are inclined to talk about it in a different way. We tell a different story, one in which sustainability is most often thought to be mechanical, no more than environmental management and, in that, principally concerned with energy efficiency and carbon management. According to this account, sustainability is concerned with quantities – the physical and measurable aspects of matters such as climate change, energy consumption, carbon footprints, transport and the performance of buildings and materials. All of this is important, but as the story of Aphrodite shows us, it is not enough. The older myth presents harmony (of which sustainability is a part) as having a much wider and deeper meaning, setting it within not just measurement and a narrow economy, but within Love as the ground of all being, suggesting that our economic, environmental and social lives are connected and cannot be sensibly considered apart from each other; that life, if you like, is about relationships; loving relationships, a continuous and integrated mutuality and reciprocity, which, in Aphrodite's story, is called Harmonia or Harmony.

We can see that the story of Aphrodite encourages us to probe beneath and beyond the conventional discussion of sustainability to reveal that upon which it depends. In the face of our present difficulties – of which climate collapse, resource depletion, economic disruption and global poverty are, perhaps, the most evident – the story urges us to see that sustainability cannot be understood, let alone achieved, by a narrow focus on technology or by a mere pruning of the outlying branches of convention. If we are going to avoid what must at least be the possibility of a mighty catastrophe we have to examine this matter at its roots. In doing so, we have to return to that which, in truth, we know but may have forgotten. For there is, here, a direct and ancient relationship of cause and effect, and when we examine it without the fetter of convention, we shall see that we have not come to be where we are by accident but as a result of our own ignorance and thoughtlessness. And the reason that we have such difficulty in knowing what it is that we must now do is because we are looking for answers in the wrong place. Love matters. Listen to the voice of Love.

As a summary, let me offer some conclusions:

1. The principles of Harmony upon which so much of the work of The Prince of Wales is founded, are themselves rooted in a view of the world as interconnected and entangled. They reflect timeless and universal principles of balance, order and proportion – as represented in sacred geometry.

2. Within this thesis lies The Prince's notion of 'a crisis of perception' leading to, and at the same time brought about by, a loss of Harmony extending to all social, environmental and economic relationships.

3. The importance of 'perception' has ancient roots, not least in the Buddhist tradition, where how we perceive is the foundation of thought and hence action. And it is of vital importance when we wish to challenge a dominant convention, such as the one that most shapes our lives – the convention of patriarchy, the convention of the Liberal Market Economy.

4. My own work proposes an alternative root principle – that 'Love Is!' – that all that is when it is most true is shaped by the energetic force of Love. Such a proposition shapes all our relationships – economy, society and environment.

5. In the end, we are shaped by the stories we are told and choose to tell. We stand between an old and largely discredited story and a new and more harmonious one that is waiting to be heard and expressed. The New Story is likely to be very different from the Old Story, and in waiting upon it and seeking to tell it, we should choose Love and not Fear as our guide. For me, this is the way of Harmony.

 Principles of Harmony

At the root of Harmony lies the principle of order and proportion, that the cosmos is ordered, harmonious. Beyond our own making is eternal law, the order of Nature. Some notion of an ordered cosmos is common to all human societies, and albeit that their expressions of this order may vary, there is a common acceptance of wholeness, that there is a whole of which we are but a part. The narrative of Harmony supposes that no part can be considered other than within the whole. Many will also claim that the cosmos is purposeful, it is ordered and purposeful, that purpose being the fulfilment of itself as a whole, that it may blossom and be fruitful, although most would accept that this purpose is difficult if not impossible to discern.

In the text prepared for the third volume of the archive of his speeches and articles,[21] 'The Grammar of Harmony',[22] His Royal Highness The Prince of Wales talked of a universal geometry of circles, squares and triangles that underlies the design of traditional carpets, windows, mosques, cathedrals and temples. He also spoke of the ratios found in music and in the spiral, the Golden Ratio of Fibonacci 1, 2, 3, 5, 8, 13, which is also shown in the vortex of water. He said:

> The grammar of Harmony is therefore the grammar that underpins the structure and growth of all things in the natural world, and we resonate with these patterns because they are our patterns too – we are made up of them, just as every tree, plant and flower is made up of them.[23]

In a paper prepared for the website of the Harmony Project,[24] the Director of The Prince's Foundation's School of Traditional Arts, Khaled Azzam, said:

> [Harmony] is the Natural Order of Being which touches every aspect of our lives – physical, mental and spiritual. Every day we all witness the majesty of the rising and setting sun; we are all moved by the gentle waxing and waning of the moon and from time immemorial we have all structured our lives according to the cycle of the four seasons. That a harmony and an order exists, one which binds all creation together, we cannot deny, since as

human beings our instinct is to seek harmony – harmony in our relationships with others, harmony with our environments, and above all a harmony in ourselves which translates into the melting of the individual ego with the collective consciousness of a higher reality – a unity which holds all existence in a harmonious whole... To seek harmony means to journey inwards and outwards. To connect harmoniously with other people, to transcend historical and geographical differences, to live in respectful harmony with our environment – these are aspects of the outward journey on which the health and survival of humanity and our planet depend. Yet the outward journey is an extension of an inner one, which allows us to live well within ourselves and to achieve a balanced fulfilment in the mental and spiritual aspects of our lives.

So, if we take this pathway, the pathway of Harmony, we find ourselves committed to the practice of living harmoniously, of respecting, and aligning ourselves to, the rhythms and patterns of Nature. This is an eternal pathway ancient and utterly of our time. This pathway is necessary for us to live well and in relation to everything that is.

Principles of Harmony

Endnotes

1. *The Harmony Debates: Exploring a Practical Philosophy for a Sustainable Future*, edited by Nicholas Campion, Sophia Centre Press, 2020.

2. Ibid. 43.

3. Ibid. 21.

4. *Speeches and Articles of His Royal Highness The Prince of Wales 1968-2012*, selected and compiled by Suheil Bushrui and David Cadman, University of Wales Press, 2014; and *Speeches and Articles of His Royal Highness The Prince of Wales 2013-2017*, selected and compiled by David Cadman, University of Wales Press, 2019.

5. Ibid, Volume 3, 11.

6. Ibid. 14.

7. Ibid. 15.

8. Ibid. Volume 2, 615.

9. Ibid. Volume 1, x.

10. Ibid. Volume 3, 16-17.

11. Ibid. Volume 1, 1.

12. Ibid. Volume 3, 369.

13. *Why Love Matters: Values In Governance*, Eds. Scherto Gill and David Cadman, Peter Lang, 2015.

14.   Joseph Milne, *Metaphysics and the Cosmic Order*, Temenos Academy, 2008.

15.   Joseph Milne, *The Mystical Cosmos*, The Temenos Academy, 2013.

16.   Joseph Milne, *Metaphysics and the Cosmic Order*, Temenos Academy, 2008, 19.

17.   Op cit, Joseph Milne, 2013, 2-10.

18.   Ibid. 10.

19.   Ibid. 13.

20.   Ibid. 14.

21.   *Speeches and Articles 2013-2017*, edited by David Cadman, Wales University Press, 2019.

22.   Ibid. 10-17.

23.   Ibid. 15.

24.   theharmonyproject.org.uk. This paper is no longer listed on the site but is to be listed on the website of the University of Wales Trinity Saint David's Harmony Institute.

Principles of Harmony

CHAPTER NINE

The Tao and the I Ching

In exploring possible pathways, we now come to two ancient but utterly relevant teachings for our troubled time: The Tao and the I Ching.

The Tao

I have several translations of The Tao and two of my favourites are the translation by Stephen Mitchell[1] and the one by Ursula K. Le Guin.[2] Others that I have enjoyed are those by Ellen M. Chen,[3] which is scholarly with lots of notes and comments, and, most recently, one by Rosemarie Anderson, which is of special interest to me since she sets the Tao within the realm of the Divine Feminine.

In Mitchell's translation, the opening stanza of the Tao Te Ching, says:

> The tao that can be told
> is not the eternal Tao.
> The name that can be named
> is not the eternal Name.[5]

And Ursula Le Guin's version of this is:

> The way you can go
> isn't the real way.
> The name you can say
> isn't the real name.[6]

At once I am caught off guard, for my own Western culture insists on naming and knowing, on possessing and controlling. What can I do?

Well, I can listen and explore.

For me, The Tao is the most wonderful expression of wholeness and connection, of relationship, and it is a teaching that honours the darkness, which Ursula Le Guin calls the mystery and the hidden. Stephen Mitchell translates it as follows:

> Yet mystery and manifestations
> arise from the same source.

This source is called darkness.

Darkness within darkness.
The gateway to all understanding.[7]

By contrast to the Christian, and indeed the Quaker, emphasis on The Light, darkness as the gateway to all understanding is exactly what I have found, and to find it expressed in this way is very reassuring. Rosemarie Anderson translates it as follows:

Dark beyond dark is
The door to all subtleties.[8]

Dark beyond dark. That's it.

The Tao is thought to have been written down in China by Lao-Tzu some time in the last five hundred years BC. Nothing much is known about Lao-Tzu, but he was probably the archive-keeper of one of the small kingdoms of his time,[9] and he may have been an older contemporary of Confucius. Some regard the verses as a treatise on the art of government,[10] whilst others find them to be more of a philosophy of life. In any event, The Tao offers a way of perceiving ourselves and our relationships with each other that is quite contrary to present Western culture. It is not, as is sometimes supposed, simply a treatise on not-doing, not at all, rather it is a teaching of doing in ways that are integrated and selfless, where "we can't tell the dancer from the dance."[11] There is a softness and a gentleness to the teachings, but also a strength and a firmness, and of all the great world religions, says Stephen Mitchell, "the teaching of Lao-Tzu is by far the most female."[12] Here it is in his description of the Tao:

The Tao is called the Great Mother:
empty yet inexhaustible,
it gives birth to infinite worlds.[13]

And Rosemarie Anderson, who, in her early thirties, travelled to Asia and studied the etymology of Chinese characters, says this:

To my surprise, I discovered that the Tao was profoundly *feminine*! Never could I have predicted that because, in the English translations I read, the Tao is commonly referred to as 'It' throughout the poems. How could so many translators, almost all men, not have noticed that the Tao is consistently referred to as 'mother', 'virgin', and 'womb of creation', all of which are clearly feminine and hardly gender neutral?... I could not possibly refer to the Tao as anything other than 'She'.[14]

And later, in a section titled 'The Divine Feminine Tao', she says:

The tenderness and hiddenness of the Tao signal Her Feminine nature... Not only is the Tao's nature uniquely feminine, but creation is described as a solo act rooted in the immortal void, the dark womb. Endlessly returning to source, all creation passes through her womb and then into the world.[15]

The book of the Tao is composed of eighty-one 'chapters', each of which is made up of a small number of short verses or stanzas, and the text presents verse after verse that challenge our present instrumental and controlling mode of being. It suggests a more receptive mode, a discipline perhaps, of surrender and attentiveness:

Therefore the Master
acts without doing anything
and teaches without saying anything.
Things arise and she lets them come;
things disappear and she lets them go.
She has but doesn't possess,
acts but does not expect.
When her work is done, she forgets it.
That is why it lasts forever.[16]

Leadership is said to require a care of those who are led, without the pomp of authority. It is service to others: "Do your work and then step back. The only path to serenity." It offers virtues of simplicity and generosity

In dwelling, live close to the ground.
In thinking, keep it simple.
In conflict be fair and generous.
In governing, don't try to control.
In work, do what you enjoy.
In family life, be completely present.[18]

Another feature of the text is the apparent paradox in which opposites are resolved into complementarities:

There is a time for being ahead,
a time for being behind;
a time for being in motion,
a time for being at rest;
a time for being vigorous,
a time for being exhausted;
a time for being safe,
a time for being in danger.[19]

Or these:

If you want to shrink something,
you must first let it expand.
If you want to get rid of something,
you must first allow it to flourish.
If you want to take something,
you must first allow it to be given.
This is called the subtle perception
of the way things are.

The soft overcomes the hard.
The slow overcomes the fast.[20]

The Tao never does anything,
yet through it everything is done.[21]

Yielding not dominating is the way of the Tao,[22] it nourishes and completes all things.[23] As Ursula Le Guin has it:

The Way is hidden
in its namelessness.
But only the Way
begins, sustains, fulfils.[24]

And there is always integration: for when male and female combine, all things achieve harmony. I note that these words are akin to the later gnostic teachings in the *Gospel of Thomas*, that "when you make the female into a single One so that the male is not the male and the female is not the female...then you will enter the Kingdom."[26]

The Tao is the mother of all things:

The Tao gives birth to all beings,
nourishes them, maintains them,
cares for them, comforts them, protects them,
takes them back to itself,
creating without possessing,
acting without expecting,
guiding without interfering.
That is why love of the Tao
is the very nature of things.[27]

And she is at ease:

The Tao is always at ease.
[She] overcomes without competing,
answers without speaking a word,
arrives without being summoned,
accomplishes without a plan.[28]

The Tao is full of compassion:

I have just three things to teach:
simplicity, patience, compassion.[29]

In these ways, and of course in so much more, this ancient teaching directly challenges those things we have come to believe to be true, those things that have shaped our language and our ways of being: consumption and greed give way to simplicity; pace and competition give way to patience; control and aggression give way to compassion; opposites are resolved in their complementarity; the soft overcomes the hard.

And for the purpose of this book, moving on from what we discovered in Chapter 7, partnership and relational being, The Tao offers another language, a language of integration, connection and relationship. And as I read it, in its many versions, I begin to see that the Tao is Love. There is nothing that can be said about the Tao since the Tao is beyond words, and the same can be said of Love. In such a place, we come to Silence, resting there and watching Love flow through us. For me, Love is the energy of the Tao, or rather it is the movement of the Tao, from and to. Or… But then we are caught once more in words.

So, if now we are told by science that everything that is is interconnected and part of a whole, our world, the universe, the cosmos, then the whole is the Tao and the fabric of the interconnection is Love, the weave, the flow of waters from a divine spring, running through streams and rivers back to the ocean of Oneness. From Oneness comes Twoness, the *yin* and *yang* that form the apparent opposition before the coming of Threeness, reconciliation through Love, and the arising of all that is:

> Man follows the earth.
> Earth follows the universe.
> The universe follows the Tao.
> The Tao follows only itself.[30]

To which I would say:

> And the following is Love,
> And that which follows is Love.

Only in Love can the Path of the Tao be discerned, be known, and, as a wave, become manifest in the energy of life, expressed in

Nature. Look all around you. Listen to the Silence in the night, for it is from the Darkness that Light arises. And as soon as Love is named it has gone, back into the darkness from whence it came. Following on from what we discovered in Chapter 2, and inspired by the Tao, I would say this:

> Follow with love,
> but do not follow.
> Love is always waiting for you.
> There in the darkness.
>
> Make some tea.
> Offer it to a friend,
> and set it down.
> Ask her:
> "Would you like cake?"
>
> Everything is Love.
> And Love is nowhere to be seen.
>
> The tide is rising and falling.
> The moon grows large and small.
> The sun arises from the East,
> and sets in the West.
> The breeze runs through the reed bed.
>
> Love at work.

The I Ching

I began to write this on an auspicious day, the 1st February, the Celtic feast day of Imbolc, when the first lambs are born and when snowdrops and aconites are in flower. Somewhat awkwardly, I think, this became the Christian festival of Candlemas, but in the ancient Chinese teaching of the I Ching, this time of the year is represented by the twenty-fourth Hexagram, *Fu*, which means Turning Point, the time in which the light returns. The nurturing darkness of Winter gives birth once more to the light, and movement begins from the feminine qualities of *yin* to the masculine qualities of *yang*.[31] But, as I say this, I must also say that beyond these notions of the feminine and the masculine is an ungendered realm of qualities of which I will speak later. And please note that I do not claim scholarship. My writing is not of this kind. At my age, I don't have the muscle tone for scholarship. Rather I want to share what I have come across and what I have made of it, what it has said to me, in the hope that you will set off on your own adventures, perhaps be tempted to make your own enquiries and, no doubt, come to your own conclusions.

So here we are in February as the darkness begins to bring forth the light. This is a special time of the year for me, for all those years ago I was born from the darkness of my mother's belly into the darkness of early December, as the dying light moved towards the Winter solstice. And then, before I was one month old, the year had turned, as the darkness once more began to give birth to the light. Perhaps this is why I have come to feel that darkness is misunderstood. In many cultures and, especially in many Western religious teachings, it is described as a place we should move away from, a lower realm that we should transcend in order to reach the higher realm of light. It is even assumed to be associated with evil and, of course, with death. This is not how it is for me, and I note that in the Celtic tradition, the day, or the month, or the year, always started in darkness – the evening gave rise to the following day, the dark phase of the moon gave birth to the new moon, the feast of Samhain, on the first of November, began the year as the light yielded to darkness. In this way, everything began by entering the darkness, and the light always arose out of darkness. This seems to me to be evidently true. It is in the darkness that healing and transformation take place. The seed falls into the earth as the light gives way to darkness, and in the darkness it is transformed into a shoot, which remains in the nurturing darkness of the soil ready to come forth as the light returns. It is not the light but the darkness that gives it birth.

Over time, in the last millennium or so BC, the teachings of the I Ching were systematised into a series of trigrams and hexagrams, based upon solid and broken lines, the solid line being *yang* (masculine, odd numbers) and the broken line being *yin* (feminine, even numbers). These formations were interpreted and used for guidance and divination. Remember, at this point, that the reference to masculine and feminine is not to be taken as a gendered separation of male and female. These masculine and feminine qualities are found in all of us, men and women alike. The masculine, or *yang*, qualities are referred to as Heaven and the feminine, or *yin*, qualities as Earth, the former being regarded as creative, or rather becoming manifest, and the latter as receptive. By way of integration, the manifesting *yang* falls down and into the receptive *yin*, and the *yin* rises up towards the *yang* – in all of us and in all that is.

The hexagrams are constructed by either the casting of yarrow sticks or the casting of three coins to decide whether the lines are to be odd or even. In the casting of the coins, which is the method I have used, heads might be taken as a three and tails as a two, and the lines are combinations of the count of the casting of the coins, giving the necessary odd or even totals.

The first hexagram of the I Ching is *Ch'ien*,[33] which is said to be The Creative. It is represented as six solid lines, one on top of the other, two trigrams, one above the other:

It is an expression of *yang* and represents the primal power, which is light-giving, active, strong and of the spirit. It is conceived as motion, both in the cosmos and in each one of us. In the coming together of the two trigrams, its image is Heaven above and below.

The course of the Creative alters and shapes beings until each attains its true specific nature, then it keeps them in conformity with Great Harmony.[34]

In its qualities of 'sublime' and 'success' it is connected to Love:

To sublimity, which, as the fundamental principle, embraces all other attributes, it links love. To the attribute success are linked the mores, which regulate and organise the expression of love and thereby makes them successful.[35]

And through 'furthering' and 'perseverance' it is connected to justice and wisdom.[36] This link between love, justice and wisdom is of great importance to us at a time when justice is so often separated from love and wisdom and all too often expressed assertively as little more than a bundle of rights.

Because the first line (the bottom line) of *Ch'ien* is a nine (cast as three heads in the casting of the coins), it is what is termed a change line, which means that after the first divination or guidance it has then to be read again, this time with a broken, feminine, line at the bottom.

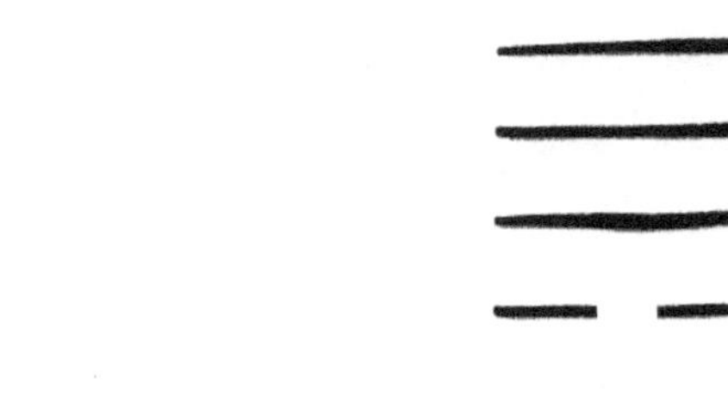

Now it is *Kou*,[37] Coming to Meet, which indicates that although, at high Summer, the darkness of *yin*, has been altogether eliminated, "furtively and unexpectedly"[38] it begins to rise again from within and below. Eventually, as the number of broken *yin* lines of darkness increase in number from below, all the solid lines of light are replaced, and we return to the darkness of Winter.

This hexagram is now made of six broken lines and is the second hexagram, *K'un*,[39] which is called The Receptive:

Now, it represents the utter dark, yielding, receptive power of *yin*. Its image is Earth.

However, the first line of *K'un* is again a change line, being made of three twos, and so when it is reversed it becomes *Fu*, which is called The Turning Point.[40]

Fu is called The Turning Point because now the time of utter darkness is past, and the light is returning. In December-January, the days lengthen, shown as the light of *yang* begins to increase from the bottom of the hexagrams upwards.

Between the depths of Winter and high Summer, or in the movement from utter darkness to full light, we have in-between times. In February-March, when the light is moving upwards and the darkness is declining, we have the hexagram *T'ai*,[41] judged to be a time of Peace. This is a time when the influences are said to be in harmony.[42]

The Tao and the I Ching

In August-September, we see in the hexagram *P'i*,[43] the upward movement of darkness, which is said to be a time of standstill and decline, a time that is judged to be Stagnation, a time when it is said that heaven and earth are out of communion.[44]

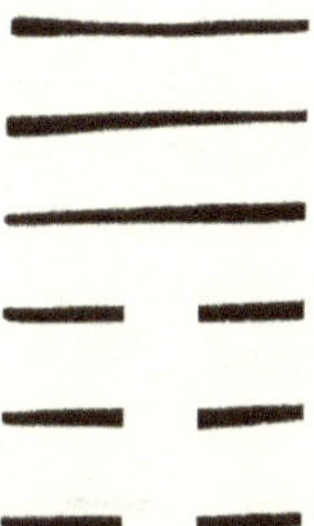

At first sight, and worryingly for me, it would seem that light is taken as being more propitious than darkness. For if this was not the case, why would *P'i*, Hexagram 12, moving to darkness, be more harshly presented than *T'ai*, Hexagram 11, moving to light – why would one be called Stagnation and the other Peace?

But perhaps there is another reading and what follows is no more than my own interpretation of the hexagrams as described by Richard Wilhelm and C. F Baynes but now linked to the Celtic wheel of the year – which I have described in my story 'The King Who Lost his Memory' set out in the Appendix to *Love and the Divine Feminine* – which is evident in the ever-flowing, and seasonal, a movement from darkness to light and from light to darkness.

Consider this.

Full light, the summer solstice (Hexagram 1), begins to give way to rising darkness (Hexagrams 44 and 33). At the autumn equinox (Hexagram 12) there is a momentary pause. But it is only momentary as the darkness continues to rise until, at winter solstice (Hexagram 2) it has entirely received or taken in the weakening light. In this state, in this darkness and within the earth, the light rests, is healed and transformed so that as it rises (Hexagrams 24 and 19) and the new shoots begin to appear, snowdrops and crocus, until at the spring equinox (Hexagram 11) all is once more in balance, reinvigorated and full of the potential for its flourishing. Thus, it proceeds with rising light (Hexagrams 34 and 43) until we come, again, to the summer solstice. From there, once more, it returns.

Perhaps this movement of darkness and light is what brings life, born in the incarnation of light through the belly of Mother Earth. Without this, the creative or manifesting light of Heaven cannot be brought to life on Earth, is unable to be born and reborn.

But however this might be, we must see that, at all times, the feminine and masculine energies are moving, never static. As the Buddha said: coming to be coming to be, ceasing to be ceasing to be. By way of example, this interplay of the feminine and masculine is shown in the sixteenth hexagram, Yü, which is called Enthusiasm[45]

Here, the feminine *yin* is held in the fourth line from the bottom by the masculine *yang*, which binds the feminine together, but is yet supported by the feminine. The upper trigram is thunder, and the lower the earth, so the energy of thunder arises from the midst of receptivity of the earth:

When, at the beginning of summer, thunder – electrical energy – comes rushing forth from the earth again, and the first thunderstorm refreshes nature, a prolonged state of tension is resolved. Joy and relief make themselves felt.... The enthusiasm of the heart expresses itself involuntarily in a burst of song, in dance and rhythmic movement of the body. From immemorial times the inspiring effort of the invisible sound that moves all hearts, and draws them together, has mystified mankind.[46]

In this way the sky and the earth are connected in the lightning and the thunder, the predominant darkness of the feminine and of the earth uniting with a single charge of light, the masculine, and from this great energy, enthusiasm, erupts. This kind of mysterious and yet evident integration of the masculine and feminine energies, so difficult to describe in Western language, is expressed throughout the I Ching and challenges us to question all that we know about the apparent opposition of the feminine and the masculine, about the apparent opposition of darkness and light. In a way, it releases us from the limitations of our language and offers us myriad possibilities for integration. Both darkness and light come alive.

> I said to my soul, be still, and wait without hope
> For hope would be hope for the wrong thing; wait without love
> For love would be love of the wrong thing; there is yet faith
> But the faith and the love and hope are all in the waiting.
> Wait without thought, for you are not yet ready for thought:
> So the darkness shall be the light and the stillness the dancing.
>
> Whisper of running streams. And winter lightening,
> The wild strawberry unseen and the wild strawberry,
>
> T. S Eliot, East Coker, *The Four Quartets*.[47]

The next task, for me, not here but in time to come, will be to express this movement of darkness and light without any reference of 'the feminine' and 'the masculine'; to find an ungendered form of expression that simply refers to this in terms of qualities.

Endnotes

1.   Lao-Tzu, *Tao Te Ching: The Book of the Way*, translated by Stephen Mitchell, Kyle Cathie, 1988.

2.   Lao-Tzu, *Tao Te Ching: A Book About The Way and the Power of the Way*, translated by Ursula K. Le Guin, Shambala, 1998.

3.   *The Tao Te Ching: A New Translation with Commentary*, translated by Ellen M. Chen, Paragon House, 1989.

4.   *The Divine Feminine Tao Te Ching: A New Translation & Commentary*, translated by Rosemarie Anderson, Inner Traditions, 2021.

5.   Op cit, Stephen Mitchell, Chapter 1.

6.   Op cit, Ursula K. Le Guin, Chapter 1.

7.   Op cit. Stephen Mitchell, Chapter 1.

8.   Op cit, Rosemarie Anderson, Chapter 1.

9.   Op cit, Stephen Mitchell, vii.

10.   Ibid.

11.   Ibid.

12.   Ibid. ix.

13.   Ibid. Chapter 6.

14.	Op cit, Rosemarie Anderson, 3.

15.	Ibid. 11.

16.	Op cit, Stephen Mitchell, Chapter 2.

17.	Ibid. Chapter 9.

18.	Ibid. Chapter 8.

19.	Ibid. Chapter 29.

20.	Ibid. Chapter 36.

21.	Ibid. Chapter 37.

22.	Ibid. Chapter 40.

23.	Ibid. Chapter 41.

24.	Op cit, Ursula K. Le Guin, Chapter 41.

25.	Op cit, Stephen Mitchell, Chapter 42.

26.	*The Gospel of Thomas*, translated by Jean-Yves Leloup and translated into English by Joseph Rowe, Inner Traditions, 1986, 19.

27.	Op cit, Stephen Mitchell, Chapter 51.

28.	Ibid. Chapter 73.

29.   Ibid. Chapter 67.

30.   Op cit, Stephen Mitchell, Chapter 25.

31.   There are a number of editions of the I Ching but the one
        that I have used is the one translated by Richard Wilhelm
        and translated into English by C. F. Baynes. It was first
        published in 1950, but my copy is a later edition that was
        published in 1997. It has a Preface by Carl Jung.

32.   This story is told as the story of The King Who Lost His
        Memory in the Appendix of my book, *Love and the Divine
        Feminine*, published by Panacea Books in 2020.

33.   Op cit, Richard Wilhelm, 3, Hexagram 1.

34.   Ibid.5.

35.   Ibid. 5-6.

36.   Ibid. 6.

37.   Ibid. 170, Hexagram 44.

38.   Ibid. 170.

39.   Ibid 10, Hexagram 2.

40.   Ibid. 97, Hexagram 24.

41.   Ibid. 48, Hexagram 11.

42.   Ibid. 48.

43.   Ibid. 52, Hexagram 12.

The Tao and the I Ching

44.   Ibid. 52.

45.   Ibid. 67.

46.   Ibid. 68.

47.   T.S. Eliot, East Coker, *Four Quartets*, Faber and Faber, Tenth impression, 1979, 24-25.

CHAPTER TEN

The Economy of Love

I n the Preface to *Love and the Divine Feminine*,[1] Love says:

"Great Love is an old and lost language. And in your time, being little understood, it is difficult to speak of. Yet without Great Love nothing can be truly understood or said.

"In your disconnected world, you need to know this. Separated and apart, you find no place for me. Seeking only to have and then to have more, you find no place for me. In your greed and your violence, you find no place for me. But without me, everything disintegrates and cannot be reunited with the One."

Suppose then for a moment that this urging of Love is true. Suppose for a moment, at this particular time and in every place, that we are being asked to become more truly ourselves, to shun fear and to love one another. Suppose that from some deep place within and beyond, and in response to our evident degradation of Nature, and the damaging rise of our greed and violence, we are being asked to turn and take another path – the path that returns us to our true Being, being within Nature, following the path of Love. To what extent would this challenge our present ways of being? Could we ask this question: if Love is to arise within us, how shall we be?

Those who have loved deeply, who have been deeply in love, will have some sense of what Love feels like. If they have loved completely, without condition – if they have dwelt in Love's realm – they will know the utter surrender it requires. When this happens, we become part of that Divine Love which is in all that is; for such Love is both within us and beyond us; and it is both universal and eternal. Whether or not we see it and feel it, it is ever-present, ever moving and waiting to be manifest in all being, in all Nature.

Yes, you might say, we know that, but what about 'the real world'? To which I say, wait a moment: suppose that instead of

The Economy of Love

taking it to be a platitude, we were to recognise it as the most vital and in-forming principle of Being. Suppose we understood it to shape all that truly is. How then would we proceed? How then would we be and what would we do in all the heavenly and mundane aspects of our lives? If Love is present in all that is, it must be present in our everyday experience. It must be more than an idea. It must work.

Suppose we take our present 'reality' head on. Suppose we take Love to be the essential underlying principle shaping that most dominant phenomenon of our time – our economy. Now that would, 'put a cat amongst the pigeons' but just for the moment let's see where this would take us.

It is easy to assume that when there is talk of 'the economy' it must be about something absolute, something like gravity, something with seemingly unquestionable laws that have to be obeyed. This is an illusion. There is no absolute form of economy, only differing economies that arise from the different principles and values that underpin them. And if a particular economy – like ours – is in disarray, then it is likely that there is something wrong, not simply with its technical operation but with its root principles and values.

The economy that has shaped our lives for the last fifty (and certainly the last twenty) or so years is one that has, of course, delivered much for many if not enough for all. But it is flawed – for it is an economy that is based upon some very strange and, as it happens, false principles. Founded upon Adam Smith's notion of 'enlightened self-interest', it assumes that if each one of us acts entirely selfishly then the wellbeing of all will be delivered. Oddly, you might think, personal selfishness is supposed to deliver communal wellbeing. This is an economy of separation.

This economy, this 'old economy', as we should now think of it, also assumes that 'growth' is always good; and that whatever the limits and whatever the costs, growth will always deliver wellbeing. Indeed, it assumes that it is only growth that can do this – albeit that this growth is dependent upon high levels of what we now know to be unsustainable borrowing, and, more importantly, of an unsustainable and highly damaging exploitation of Nature. It is an economy of dogma in which growth has become not a means but a necessary end. This is an economy that insists upon having and then having more, without end, without limit.

Those who defend this old economy as the only one that is possible, may sound confident and persuasive but, in truth, they must surely now explain how it is that it has gone so badly wrong – not just a little wrong but spectacularly wrong; and we must be prepared to challenge their convention – to ask if the emperor really has any clothes on.

For example, how is it that above a certain level of need the evidence seems to suggest there is no positive correlation between increasing economic growth and increasing wellbeing? How is it that the gap between those who have more than enough and those who have too little has not diminished, but has increased – ever wider? How is it that this old economy, with its addiction to debt, in 2008/2009 all but destroyed Western society and brought great enterprises and even nations to their knees? And if it is so robust, why, in the UK, did it need to be supported with a subsidy of £375 billion – over £14,000 for each family in the UK, given to the very banks that brought about the collapse? What kind of 'reality' is this?

In truth, an economy is an organism; it is something that is alive and never quite still, always moving, rising and falling towards and away from an equilibrium upon which it never rests. Like the coming and going of the seasons or the rise and fall of the tide, this constant undulation is natural, endemic and not to be feared. From time to time, however, a distorted economy can become so strained and troubled, so overblown, that it crashes and breaks or it can be disturbed by events beyond its control, such as Covid 19 – for it is always more vulnerable than it cares to admit. And,

 The Economy of Love

when this happens, the damage may take a long time to mend. This is where we are now. BUT although business and political leaders may try to drag the economy back to where it was, the point we have to note is this: in its distress and disruption the economy is not striving to regain its old form. It seeks not 'a return to normal' but a transformation. Those who choose only to live in the old economy will deny this and will not be able to find the words to describe its reformation. They will, for example, quiver at the threat of what they will call a 'recession', when this may well be an economy naturally reforming – or rather transforming – to levels of consumption and activity that are more bearable, more sustainable.

At such a time, stillness and listening can be very helpful, for instead of the general wailing and gnashing of teeth, we can engage in quiet reflection, seeking to understand the new economy, aligning ourselves to its emerging form and enabling its coming – seeking to find our way through Love, since Love is the root of all that is. Love is the foundation of the True and the Good, the essence of True Being. Love is the wind within the wind, the breath within the breath, the economy within the economy. And we only see things as separate and apart because that is how we have learnt to see them. Almost without knowing we have come to suppose that we observe the world as 'outside' rather than experience it within.

And so the questions we might ask are these: What form will the new economy take, and can we help to shape it? And in this, what has Love to say? What might we do to bring about an Economy of Love?

At present, of course, whilst we cannot tell for certain what the new economy will be like, we can be sure it will, in time, be different from the old economy. Given the catastrophic financial and economic collapse that followed on from the banking crisis of 2007-2009, and now the global disruption of Covid 19 and its many variants, it could be very different indeed; but to reach a better understanding, we will have to free ourselves from old prejudices and habits. We have to do this and we have to have the courage to believe in the possibility of something better, something, for example, that reflects principles and values of simplicity, compassion and care for others. To do otherwise would be to surrender to a form of tyranny – a tyranny of ideas, a tyranny of perception that would close off all other possibilities and return us to the very imperfection, imbalance and injustice from which we seek to move.

And we have to do this despite seeing (or, perhaps, because of seeing) that the world of commerce and banking, and the politics of economy, seem to have changed so little since the crisis of 2008/2009. The realm in which bankers live seems to ordinary people like you and me to be a world of make-believe. Despite the fact that we saved them, they seem disinclined to say either 'sorry' or 'thank you'. They seem to have no sense of how extraordinary their world is; they seem content with business as usual. Our sense of confusion may arise from our failure to understand fully the fetter and power of convention; to see how impregnable is the realm of convention; to understand that those who 'own' convention seldom find it necessary to justify what they think and do, because they assume it is taken as a given. We may also fail to understand the law of consequences – that particular thoughts give rise to particular outcomes; that without changing perceptions we will return inevitably to where we were. In government and most of commerce there is no change of perception, only a sense that to put things right we should continue as we were with some minor adjustments. We must always return to the dogma of growth, we must return to the dogma of debt, we must accept the dogma of 'too big to fail'.

So, my dear readers, as one possible exercise, let us for a moment suppose that the new economy could be, must be, profoundly different from the old one and that it could be, must be, informed

The Economy of Love

by Love. If the old economy was shaped by selfishness and indebtedness, by addicted consumers with the need to have, and to have without limit, an Economy of Love will surely speak of something else. For, of their very nature, the principles, or rather, the qualities of Love arise from another realm: a place of integration, relationship and a caring for each other, for community and for Nature herself. The economy to which Love will give shape is therefore going to be markedly different: by the very nature of Love, it will be characterised by generous and caring relationships:

- If the old economy is about an addiction to growth, the economy of Love will be about steadiness and sufficiency – an economy of enough.

- If the old economy denies limits to growth, the economy of Love will accept working within them, seeking to integrate, sustain and enliven society, environment and economy together.

- If the old economy is about indebtedness, the economy of Love will be about thriftiness and keeping borrowing in check, wary of the bondage and burden of debt.

- If the old economy is about globalisation, the economy of Love, needing to work with relationships that are more personal and full of care, will be more about localism and regionalism.

- If the old economy is about selfishness and conflict, the economy of Love will be about compassion and co-operation.

- If the old economy is about grotesque inequalities of work and wealth, the economy of Love will be about much greater economic and social justice, an alignment of being and goodness.

- If the old economy reifies the individual, the economy of Love will nurture the individual-in-community.

- If the old economy sees Nature as a resource to be used without regard, the economy of Love will work for the well-being of Nature as a whole.

And if we are told this is just wishful thinking, we should remember that whilst we may have a lot to learn, the guardians of the old economy – who will no doubt be our critics – are not in much of a position to tell us what to do, for their economy is broken. We must remember this and have the courage to keep telling ourselves that as all economies reflect particular principles and values, we can, if we wish, build an economy on good principles, on Love.

This new economy will, of course, have to take account of limits to growth. It will have to take account of climate breakdown and resource depletion – for, in truth, the economy dwells within the environment and is dependent upon it, and not the other way around. It will have to envisage a post-fossil-fuel society. It will have to face up to global and local shortages of food and water and the recurrent possibility of pandemics. And post COP26, it is clear that it will have to be an economy that can operate within the predicament of Plus 2°C. But most especially, all of this means it will be an economy that asks us to reconsider who is our neighbour. Faced with these challenges, how could a sustainable and loving economy be other than diametrically opposed to the old economy of selfishness, consumption, waste and injustice?

I would like to suggest that the Economy of Love will be good; and by this I mean that common goodness of which Thomas Aquinas spoke, a goodness that is as natural as it is all-pervading; a goodness that is within all that is; a goodness that will, if we but align ourselves to it, bring us to that Divine Goodness that some call God – and I call Love. And if the economy is to be good it can only be just. For, as we have found, an economy that is not just is not sustainable, since it is false. In truth, sustainability, goodness and justice are one. They dwell in the realm of Love, which is to say they dwell both within and beyond and are ever-present if we would but turn towards them.

It is at this point that many will ask: 'But what can we do?' Before I come to this, I need to say a bit more about the realm of Love.

The Economy of Love only makes sense if we take as a given that Love is; that Love is the essence of all that truly is; that Love is that which sustains the flux of all that is; moves us ever towards and within Divine Goodness; is all that is True; that we take Love seriously. I am asking you to accept not only that this is so, but also that if we proceed otherwise, we are bound to inhabit a realm of fantasy that cannot, in the end be sustained – because it is false. In this way, all thought of action, let alone any action itself, has to be preceded by a challenging clarification of perception, an insistence upon founding what is done in the Truth of Love and facing up to all that this implies.

Since transformation from one form of economy to another is somewhat uncertain, complex and probably messy, the first thing we must do is pause and reflect. Before we do anything else, we need to make an effort to try and discern what is happening in our economy now and what might happen to it the future; what are the strains and stresses seeking to pull it one way or another and can they, or should they, be resisted or nurtured; where might the emerging economy be seeking to go of itself, and what seems to be its natural inclination? We must listen. Then, and only then, will we have the understanding that will enable us, rightly, to do something else. Then, and only then, will we know what is being asked of us. I am suggesting, therefore, that for once we deliberately allow our waiting and listening to precede our doing, since nothing can arise before the possibility of its arising.

In any event, once we have better understanding, the answers to the question 'What can we do?' are likely to have many and diverse forms. For example: What can we do at home? What can we do at work? How shall we work? What can we do with our savings? What food shall we eat? How and where shall we live? Another, and more personal, way of expressing this will be to ask such questions as: What can I do as a mother, father, grandparent, teacher, carer, one who is cared for, lawyer, accountant, bus driver, shopkeeper, banker – and so on? There may be no immediate and detailed prescription, but there are questions to be asked, and, with

Love, answers will be found.

There is a growing understanding that the rules of the old economy are no longer fit for purpose. For example, in America and then in the UK, post-2008/2009 some students began to protest against lectures in classical economics based upon supposed 'efficient markets' and 'perfect competition'. They saw that such propositions bore little or no relation to what they were experiencing in their own lives. There has also been a growing discussion about what is referred to as 'solidarity economics' (activities organised to address inequalities arising from capitalist economics); interesting work has been done by the New Economics Foundation in London to bring about new and dynamic forms of economics; and there is, of course, the more established discussion of Herman Daly's steady state economics and the propositions of 'limits to growth' as presented by Donella and Dennis Meadows and as now carried forward by CASSE (steadystate.org). Much of this is captured in a most accessible book, *Enough is Enough* by Rob Dietz and Dan O'Neill – to which I will refer again in a moment – and in an excellent paper by Andrea Weber on 'Enlivenment', which can be found on the www.boell.de website.

One of the greatest obstacles to an Economy of Love is the belief that it cannot be done. Not only this, but that we should not even bother to try since we must unquestionably accept the economy we have. Many of us feel that there are people who are much more clever than we are, and who know why things are as they are. They have probably persuaded us that they live in 'the real world', and that all of our questioning and confusion is no more than private ignorance and fantasy. Indeed, this perception may be so deeply entrenched in us that even when we want to question the present economy, we remain caught in its grasp. We may feel that we are bound by its mantra of growth based upon debt, its reliance upon markets to sort out all our problems, perfectly and fairly. But there

   The Economy of Love

is another way. Instead of following the normal route of beginning by critiquing the existing economy and then trying to propose something else, we can turn the matter on its head and proceed as follows:

• Start by stating clearly what it is that we hold dear in terms of our own personal and private values; that which governs our private life.

• With these values and principles in mind, describe the forms of public governance that must flow from them.

• Within this context, go on to propose an economy that is true to these values and these forms of governance.

• Then, and only then, look to see what it is that stands in our way.

The first advantage of this route is that it places economy within society. The second advantage is that, instead of allowing the present form of economy to shape all that can be said, it is put on the defensive – as it should be.

I once followed this process with a small weekend gathering at the Quaker conference centre at Charney Manor in Oxfordshire. The experience was telling. Firstly, it was clear that those gathered together found it easy to describe the values and principles that governed their lives personally and within their immediate community. Not surprisingly they emphasised the place of love, loving-kindness, honesty and simplicity in their lives, spoke of the need for a relationship of care with the Earth, and touched upon social values, such as equality and education. However, these values were seen to be contrary to the values and principles that were thought to govern society as a whole: the conventions of consumerism, materialism and a somewhat aggressive individuality.

We discovered that this gap between personal and public values had been reported in a UK Values Survey,[2] which had found that many people shared similar personal values: caring, family, honesty, humour/fun, friendship, fairness and compassion. The survey also had gone on to report on comparable values expressed in peoples' notions of 'community life' – quality of life, family, buy local, helpfulness and friendship. But, when it came to perceived national values and forms of governance, there was a chasm. According to the survey, the perceived characteristics of national life were very different – bureaucracy, crime/violence, uncertainty about the future, corruption and blame, and concerns about drugs and alcohol abuse. Crossing this gap between the private and the public is difficult and we at Charney Manor found it difficult, too. This led us to search for more local forms of economy and governance where it would be easier to reflect personal and communal values. Indeed, it was suggested that we needed to take back to ourselves some of the responsibilities for governance that we had (knowingly or otherwise) given to others – either the state or markets. Importantly, here was the idea that markets sometimes work well, but may not always be suitable for all forms of activity, for example caring for the sick and elderly. Also important was the possibility of working outside the formal economy in neighbourhood schemes of one kind and another. And we talked about principles that would shape what we called The Good Economy – an economy that was local, just, simple, and sustainable. Standing in our way we saw not only the power of vested interests and the conventions of economic growth, indebtedness and consumerism, but also a deep sense of our own ignorance and powerlessness, feelings of isolation, fear of the unknown and not knowing who to trust; feelings of inadequacy when faced with something as apparently huge and powerful as 'the economy' and of the difficulties of becoming well-informed; the power of convention and its reluctance to change.

And here is the dilemma. As the economist Manfred Max Neef once said, the really strange thing is that in our thoughts about economy we should still be governed by ideas created in the late nineteenth century. If it was suggested that physics should still be based upon the astronomy, geology or biology of that time, it would be deemed absurd. But we seem content to take such an approach in economics.

The Economy of Love

I have already mentioned the book by Rob Dietz and Dan O'Neill, *Enough is Enough*.[3] This is a book that provides a clear overview of a different kind of economy – a Steady State Economy (SSE) – one that is not dependent on growth, reduces levels of debt and points toward greater social and economic justice. In doing this, and in presenting a number of 'strategies of enough', it follows the advice famously given by Buckminster Fuller:

> You never change things by fighting the existing reality. To change something, build a new model that makes the existing model obsolete.

Indeed, rather pleasingly, and thereby showing that these ideas of 'enough' are somewhat ancient, the authors quote Lao Tzu:

> A person who knows enough is enough will always have enough.[4]

The authors tackle questions of consumption, population growth, indebtedness, employment and inequality and provide a 'blueprint' for SSE founded upon:

> Sustainable scale, fair distribution, efficient allocation, high quality of life, improved investment, optimal labour productivity, innovative models of ownership, and environmental values.[5]

It is an economy supported by policies to:

> Limit resource use, stabilise population, distribute income and wealth equitably, reform monetary and financial systems, change the way we measure progress, secure full employment, rethink commerce, change consumer behaviour, engage politicians and the media, and improve international cooperation.[6]

The aim is to work towards "sustainable and equitable human well-being."[7]

All in all, SSE is presented as an economy that maximises its end (sustainability and equitable well-being) while economising on the ultimate sources of that wellbeing (flows of materials and energy). It is a true economy of enough. It is an economy that is based upon people consuming enough to meet their needs and leading meaningful, joyful lives, without undermining the life-support systems of the planet. It seeks to stabilise population levels and encourage families and communities to become healthy, more connected, more resilient, more neighbourly. Entrepreneurial businesses would be encouraged to provide valuable services – not just to earn a profit but improve social and environmental conditions. Cities would be redesigned, with smaller populations working and living in more compact land areas; and new forms of farming would see the elimination of the need for constantly increasing food production, lightening the impacts people have on the landscape, with less land devoted to crop production. Our lands and waters would enter a new era of healing, with energy conservation becoming a high priority as people seek ways to accomplish their goals while minimising energy inputs. Expectations about money and investment would be adjusted to match reality.

It's not such a bad vision, and surely something worth considering and understanding better. And it is worth remembering that although an Economy of Love might at first appearance seem to be unconventional, that father, or perhaps great-grandfather of modern economics, Adam Smith thought otherwise. As my colleague Scherto Gill reports in her book, *Lest We Lose Love*,[8] Adam Smith was very interested in the matter of love. The core tenet, she says of Adam Smith's *The Theory of Moral Sentiment* is love.

> To begin, Smith argues that love is an important moral sentiment in the dual dimensions in that "Man Naturally desires not only to be loved, but to be lovely." In other words, on the one hand, humans need love, love of the self, from which arises our natural yearning to pursue [the] *proper object of love*; and on the other hand, humans also aspire to be such a proper object of love.[9]

So, before we cast Love aside, even in the very 'real' and practical realm of economics, we might just reflect on the extent to which it is not the founder of this realm but our own much more recent shift in values that holds this to be absurd.

Even in this brief introduction to the possibility of an Economy of Love it is not difficult to see how such an economy relates to principles of compassion and a care of others – the work of Love. It understands relationships, whether they are between the environment, society and the economy, or between individuals, families, communities, governments and commerce. It understands the need for care and reciprocity. Nevertheless, set against these new ways of understanding economy there are powerful forces of vested interest and inertia. And so, above all else, I am suggesting that the work of Love requires a firmness of resolve, a determination not to shrug our shoulders and just be led back to the old, false and damaging economy. If the old economy is to transform into the Economy of Love, it requires attentiveness, clear listening, thorough research, clarity of thought and a persistence grounded in the perception and practice by Love.

And in this we should be encouraged. For the darkness is most evident when the light begins to arise.

Endnotes

1.   Op cit, David Cadman, 2020, 8.

2.   This was a survey undertaken by the Barratt Values Centre (valuescentre.com), but I no longer have the detailed reference.

3.   Rob Dietz and Dan O'Neill, *Enough is Enough: Building a Sustainable Economy in a World of Finite Resources*, Routledge/Earthscan, 2013.

4.   Ibid. 3.

5.   Ibid. 74.

6.   Ibid. 113.

7.   Ibid.

8.   Scherto Gill, *Lest We Lose Love: Re(dis)covering the Core of Western Culture*, Anthem Press, forthcoming 2022.

9.   Adam Smith, *The Theory of Moral Sentiments*, 1759.

Reflections

And so... if you are still here with me... I come to some reflections on the path that we have taken — starting with the matters of Language, Love and Silence; listening to the voices of women; and exploring possible future pathways. Where might this all be taking us?

My work is almost done, and I am coming to an end not only of this scribbling but also of my life. Ten years? Unlikely to be more. Could be less. Could well be less. Perhaps, then, it is not surprising that I find myself reflecting on how it is I have come to be who I am and where I am, and wondering what my purpose might have been and is now. This is a time for honesty. If some people are intrepid, I think I may be trepid. Yes, there is such a word and it means timid. I think that most of those who have known me would not suppose this was so, for I have always seemed to be easy in company and full of confidence. But now I have come to see that that is simply the part I learnt to play as a child, the cloak that over time I put on to hide my insecurity and inner anxiety when 'walking on stage'. Is it like that for all of us, or just me? I don't know. Or perhaps there is more than one part of me, one bold and outgoing and the other trepid. That could be it, too, don't you think? I don't know, and now it hardly matters.

Anyway, the 'me' that is off-stage has always been much more introverted than he has appeared to be on stage and, physically at least, the adventures that I have had have not been in wild and distant places, but close by. With London as my place of work, I have always lived more or less where I am now, first in north-east Essex, with its muddy estuaries and open farmland, and now on the coast of Suffolk, with the North Sea, the shingle beach and, best of all, the tidal river Alde. The rising and the falling of the tide lies deep within my veins. Do you know that moment when the tide turns? The very moment? It is almost impossible to see, but at one moment the boats are pointing into the full and rising tide, and in the next they have swung on their moorings and are pointing into the ebb. And you can do nothing about it, but watch. Whatever words I use to describe this are as nothing to what actually happens.

I am telling you this because, as I said in Chapter 1, I have come to know that I cannot write other than from where I am and from whoever it is I have become. I might wish to be someone else in some other place, but I am not. I am an old and damaged patriarch living by the sea and the river, with the great dish of sky overhead and the reed beds touched by the breeze, the cry of seagulls. And I say 'patriarch' because whether I like it or not, that is what I was born into, and patriarchy is who I became; mostly benign rather than malign, I hope, but patriarchy none the less. And I say damaged because that's what happens in life, the knocks and bruises damage us, don't you think?

It is from this place, on the banks of the Alde, that I have come to see that my quest for Love and the Divine Feminine has always been an essential part of my being. Although I have only really known this in my later years, I now know that for all of my life, from early childhood to becoming an old man, this has been so; it has been the search for that which has been lost, not just for me but for all of us: Love and the Divine Feminine. But here's the point. What I have only very recently understood is this: that this search has not been for some great philosophical principle (although that has been part of it), in truth it has been a search for some inner meaning and for the Great Meaning, the two are entwined one with another, they are felt as a seeking for peacefulness and oneness. In some other life, some time before, I am now certain, for my sisters in the Brahma Kumaris have told me that it is so, I lived my life not in the body of a man, as I do now, but in the body of a woman. And perhaps, or rather probably, over many lives I have lived in both, first the one and then the other in a patterned sequence. And I know that in some other time I lived with and amongst women. So, in a world dominated by men, where both Love and the Feminine have been dismissed and sometimes reviled, no wonder I have felt, and still feel, a sense of loss. Sometimes, waking in the early morning, this can be almost unbearable.

I wrote about this loss in *Love and the Divine Feminine*. And at the end of the book I asked those questions that are set out in the Introduction to this book, questions which suggest that we need to be explicit about, and attentive to, both Love and the Feminine, and that we need to open ourselves to the possibility that in trying to find our way out of the catastrophe that we are bringing upon ourselves – a toxic mixture of the degradation of Nature, climate breakdown, evident social and economic injustice, and increasing division and conflict – we need to find a different discourse and a more loving and collaborative way of being. In the end, for me at least, this requires a search for what the Buddha called *upekkhā*, equanimity, one of the four 'divine abidings' and the foundation of them all.

As I write down those words, I am conscious of their inadequacy. After all, I write 'inner meaning', not knowing at all what that might be. This inner meaning, sometimes called 'the soul', is often described as feminine, and I like that, even if the reality beyond the image is utterly mysterious and without gender. She is my *anima*, the lost feminine part of me, and perhaps of us. Lost in the dominating and damaging bondage of patriarchy, which, over many lives, has left some of us misshapen, unable to feel what many others feel, unable to feel the pain of the other. Well, perhaps not entirely, but often; caught up in our own need to have order, to be in control, not of others, but of ourselves. Isn't that what patriarchs want? Control? Dominance? That is the real damage of patriarchy, not just the evident degradation of Nature, but the more subtle damage it has brought to each one of us, each with our own particular wounds.

The writer and visionary, Anne Baring, has a chapter towards the end of her book, *The Dream of the Cosmos*,[1] in which she speaks of the transformation of the soul, which she relates to the need for a new cosmic consciousness. She says that the Cosmos "calls us to become aware that we participate in its life, that everything is sacred and connected: one life; one spirit."[2] And she adds, "Alchemy responds to that call. It asks us to develop a cosmic consciousness."[3] This might sound daunting, but to find 'another language' we have to become brave or foolish enough to explore forbidden possibilities, and an understanding of the ancient practice of Alchemy is one such. For, as the seventeenth century illustration at the beginning of Anne Baring's chapter shows, Alchemy follows in the footsteps of Nature. And as we have discovered, in the work of Harmony (see Chapter 8) we must let Nature be our teacher, rescuing the lost feminine hidden within Her and within ourselves. This is the first step of the Alchemical Great Work.[4] This is a part of our evolution:

The evolution of human consciousness on this planet is a very slow gradient of ascent from unconsciousness to self-consciousness and, ultimately, to awakened consciousness.

There are many setbacks and long periods of stagnation
and incubation. The whole of humanity suffers because the
increase of consciousness is so slow and the transformation
needed to diminish human suffering and ignorance so difficult
to implement. Now it seems that because of the turmoil in the
world and the harm to the planet caused by our unconscious
behaviour, our evolution is being accelerated, taking us to a point
where we have to make the choice between transformation and
annihilation.[5]

Carl Jung came to study alchemy, reconnecting solar, masculine,
consciousness, with lunar, feminine consciousness, redeeming the
lost aspect of spirit hidden within himself and Nature,[6] unifying
the cosmic ground,[7] reconnecting us with the ancient universal
unconscious, and reconnecting us with Wisdom, which reveals
"the fruits of a relationship with the hidden ground of life."[8]
As Anne Baring says:

Certain myths flow beneath the surface of our lives like
a mighty river, connecting our superficial awareness with
its roots, ready always when we are ready, to well up like a
perennial spring whenever we call upon our soul for help. In
European civilisation there was a wealth of ideas that had to go
underground, since they could only escape persecution by being
hidden in metaphor and allegory. Only now are they emerging,
having been preserved for the day of their 'resurrection' by a
strong mythological tradition expressed in alchemy on the one
hand and in countless legends and stories such as the fairy tale
of the Sleeping Beauty and the legend of the Holy Grail on
the other.[9]

So, what can we now say about a new myth for our time, a
Myth of Love? I think we can speak of this in two ways: we can
speak of the universal and we can speak of the everyday. Let's start
with the second of these.
Within the chapters of this book, we have, again and again,
come across suggestions for how we might live our everyday lives.
This includes the virtues set out in Chapter 2 – loving kindness,

compassion, truthfulness, patience, generosity, humility, caring for each other and for the Earth – and it includes the possibility of living within those principles of Harmony described in Chapter 8, with two Great Principles – Wholeness and Connection or, when they are brought together, Relationship. Indeed, throughout the whole of Part Three, we discovered that the only way for us to be if we are to avoid catastrophe is to live in partnership with each other and with the Earth, to live, to work, to speak, to be, always in right relation with each other and the Earth.

None of this is especially complicated, nor is it new. We have been told of this by all the great sages and spiritual traditions, our own and others. And the core discipline for such lives is the Discipline of Love, taking Love seriously and, with intent, putting it into practice in every moment of our lives. What stands in our way? Well, what stands in our way is a dominant patriarchal culture. I shall not waste my time speaking anymore about this old and now outworn kingdom. To do so will only take us back into a realm that we must leave behind. But – if we choose to leave it behind – we can speak of something else. And that's the point isn't it. That was the point of the fable of 'The Wrong Turning (Chapter 5). That is what the Old Woman said to the King:

> "The only thing for you to do," said the Old Woman, "is to care for each other and to care for the Earth as if she was your Mother. Tenderness, kindliness and care. These are the qualities that you will need both to limit as much as you can the catastrophe that will come, and then to look after each other when the storms have swept many of you away."

But did the King take her advice? Do we take her advice? Or do we turn away and say, 'It's too difficult' or 'But this is not how the world is'? As I have said again and again, the Buddha has long taught us in the opening stanza of the Dhammapada, the world is as we think it is: 'with our thoughts we make the world'. It is not that we cannot do what we now know to be true, but only that, despite the floods, the fires and the pestilence, we do not have the courage to do so. And the madness is we think that to ignore these dangers, to turn away from the Discipline of Love, is to be 'realistic'. But what is this reality that we speak of? When we see where it has taken us to, how can we say it is 'just the way things are'?

This brings us to the second way of speaking, to universal principles and ultimate truth. It brings us to what, in Chapter 2, the late John Templeton of the Templeton Foundation refers to as Love as Ultimate Reality or that of which Whitall Perry spoke in *A Treasury of Traditional Wisdom*:

> Love is the energizing elixir of the universe, the cause and effect of all harmonies, lights, brilliance and the heat in wine and fire, it is the aroma of perfumes and the breath of the Divinity: it is the Life in all being... It is all that the texts have to say, and the more that remains unspoken.[10]

Or to that which Rumi taught:

> Love makes the sea boil like a cauldron,
> Love reduces the mountains to sand.
> Love cracks hundreds of fissures into the heavens unconsciously,
> Love makes the earth tremble.
> ... (God said): "If it wasn't by pure love, how could I have brought
> the heavens into existence?
> I have elevated the sublime celestial sphere so that you could understand the sublimity of Love."[11]

If we are, here, talking of mysterious, universal principles then it would seem that we may find great delight, and certainly something more plausible than principles of accounting.

In this work, I have presented the possibility of such Another Reality – the matter of Language in Chapter 1, my own propositions in Chapters 2 and 3 of Love and of Silence as being of the essence, the voices of women in Chapters 4 to 6, the propositions of Riane Eisler/Douglas Fry and Kenneth Gergen in Chapter 7, the principles of Harmony in Chapter 8, the teachings of the Tao and the I Ching in Chapter 9, and even the possibility of an Economy of Love in Chapter 10. There is no lack of data, and there is no lack of evidence of the need for change, for urgent change. There is only a lack of belief and intention. In this sense, the dilemma we face is a spiritual crisis. What do we take to be true? Are we prepared to face that truth and act accordingly?

When Anne Baring speaks of Alchemy in Part Six of her book *The Dream of the Cosmos*,[12] she refers to the Seven Processes involved in the Alchemical Great Work. They are:

1. The rescue of the lost feminine aspect of spirit hidden within Nature and ourselves.
2. The process of transformation involved in this rescue.
3. The death of the old consciousness symbolised by the old king and queen.
4. The formation of the new consciousness symbolised by the young king and queen.
5. The formation of the Hermaphrodite – the union of the two transformed elements.
6. The integration of body, soul and spirit.
7. The union with what the alchemist called the unus mundus, the divine cosmic ground.

Perhaps we are already seeing the first three of these aspects taking place in our world, as the feminine rises and the old consciousness begins to fall apart. And then, perhaps, we can begin to see the coming of a new consciousness in which we see first the arising of the feminine and then the integration of the feminine and the masculine. This is aligned to the fourth, and fifth and sixth processes, for it seems to be closely aligned to my seeking an integration of the feminine and the masculine and, perhaps, an ungendered discourse, leading, indeed, to the arising of the soul, our inner being. Perhaps, unknowingly, and with faltering steps, I too have been on the alchemist's path seeking 'the divine cosmic ground', following in the footsteps of Nature.

Now that is a thought!

Do we need to create a space for our souls to expand into, to open their wings? Perhaps our evolutionary purpose is to learn how to participate actively in Love, to receive and give love in such a way that the order and wellbeing of the Cosmos is supported

Reflections

and nourished. Perhaps the questions we should therefore ask of ourselves and of any enterprise in which we are involved are: am I loving, are we loving? Am I/are we giving and receiving love? Is our work guided by Love? And is it an expression of Love? Are we loving one another? And are we caring for our Mother Earth?

Even in Love, this can sometimes seem to be a lonely path.

I am writing this last reflection in the aftermath of COP26, the gathering that one young woman called 'Blah, blah, blah'. And of course it is not what was promised but *what will be done* that will determine our futures, or in my case the futures of my children, my grandchildren and their children. I am struck in this by something that was a theme of Chapter 1 – the limits of language. For it seems evident to me that the reason that politicians and business leaders find it difficult to respond to the problems of climate breakdown is that they do not have the words to do so. They are quite literally lost for words. So long as they continue to envision the problems in terms of the old and degraded language of separation and conflict, solutions will evade them. The problem is not a technical problem – for there are already new ways of capturing carbon, new fuels, including hydrogen, that reduce pollution, renewable energy is on the rise and there are new forms of farming and forestry ready to be adopted for use on a large scale. The problem is not about the *mechanics*, it is about *our perception*, the *language* we use to describe what we think we must do. So long as that language remains bound in old ways of thinking we are lost. We need to be able to imagine, express and put into action entirely new ways of being. And in this, time is not on our side. Urgently, we need to tackle this matter of perception and language, for unless we can *imagine* something different, and unless we can then say what this is in a robust and practical way, we will be lost.[13]

Words create boundaries and silence breaks them down. In a world full of words, this may seem inexplicable. But it is nonetheless true, and we will only find our way in the deep silence of the soul. We need to practice silence until it becomes a part of who we are, how we listen to one another and to the Earth, how we enter into discourse. Try this. Begin and end your meetings or important conversations with a period of silence. Step into the silence and wait for the guidance that will come to you. Try not to interrupt but listen and then before you speak take another moment of silence. To return to something I have said before, *Let's take Love seriously.* Let's free ourselves to imagine a world built upon principles of Love – in detail and with intent. For there is but Love and we are made of it, made for it, made by it. It is the universal and timeless condition, the way of the Cosmos.

At the end of *Love and the Divine Feminine*, I asked a number of questions. The one question that I have as *The Recovery of Love* comes to an end is this: What needs to be in place for Love to arise? Trying to answer this question will be my next task.

Reflections

Endnotes

1. Anne Baring, *The Dream of the Cosmos: A Quest for the Soul*, Archive Publishing, 2020, Chapter 18.

2. Ibid. 457.

3. Ibid.

4. Ibid. 478.

5. Ibid. 459-460.

6. Ibid. 463.

7. Ibid.

8. Ibid. 465.

9. Ibid. 466.

10. Whitall N. Perry, *A Treasury of Traditional Wisdom*, Fons Vitae, 2000, p. 612.

11. *Mathnawi*, v. 2375 .

12. Op cit, Anne Baring, 2020.

13.   One example of this is the genre of 'ecopunk' stories that explore possible, and sometimes fantastical, futures of a surviving humankind with entirely new relationships with each other, the living world and, indeed, the cosmos. Examples include: *Ecopunk: Speculative Tales and Radical Futures*, edited by Liz Grzyb and Cat Sparks, Ticonderoga Publications, 2017, *Sunvault: Stories of Solarpunk and Eco-speculation*, edited by Phoebe Wagner and Brontë Christopher Wieland, Upper Rubber Boot, 2017, *Solarpunk: Ecological and Fantastical Stories in a Sustainable World*, edited by Gerson Lodi-Ribeiro and translated by Fabio Fernandes, World Weaver Press, 2018, *Solarpunk Summers* edited by Sarena Ulibarri, World Weaver Press, 2018, *Multispecies Cities: Solarpunk Urban Futures*, edited by Christopher Rupprecht, Deborah Cleland, Norie Tamura, Rajat Chaudhuri and Sarena Ulibarri, World Weaver Press, 2021, and *Solarpunk Winters* edited by Sarena Ulibarri, World Weaver Press, 2020.

Appendix

The Great Tree

In 2010, Jehanne De Quillan published, under the title of *The Gospel of the Beloved Companion*, what she described as a complete version of the Gospel of Mary Magdalene in which the secret teachings of Love are given to Mary by her Teacher. These teachings include a reference to a great tree, rooted in the Earth and with eight boughs that lead upwards, away from the world, in which, by passing from one to another, we may discover love and compassion, wisdom and understanding, honour and humility, strength and courage, clarity and truth, power and healing, light and goodness and, finally, grace and beauty until, freed from the world, we are embraced by a woman of extraordinary beauty, clothed in garments of white and find ourselves in a realm of blessed Silence. In doing this, in finding Love, we leave behind judgement and wrath, ignorance and intolerance, duplicity and arrogance, the weakness of the flesh, and the voice of the world.

This image is based upon this teaching and was originally drawn for me by Beth Lewis for inclusion in my book *Love and the Divine Feminine*, published in 2020 by Panacea Books.

"

www.ingramcontent.com/pod-product-compliance
Lightning Source LLC
Chambersburg PA
CBHW061423160726
47995CB00003B/726